Since John Got Sick

Since John Got Sick

A Quest for Survival and Faith

Allison Greene

John Greene

RESOURCE *Publications* · Eugene, Oregon

SINCE JOHN GOT SICK
A Quest for Survival and Faith

Resource Publications
An Imprint of Wipf and Stock Publishers
199 W. 8th Ave., Suite 3
Eugene, OR 97401

www.wipfandstock.com

PAPERBACK ISBN: 978-1-5326-5166-3
HARDCOVER ISBN: 978-1-5326-5167-0
EBOOK ISBN: 978-1-5326-5168-7

While the accounts in the upcoming pages are true, some names have been changed. Others are used with permission.

Special thanks to Wanda Owings for her editing skills and to other writers' group members: Jeanne Brooks, Deb Richardson-Moore, and Susan Simmons

Manufactured in the U.S.A.

For all the clinicians who shared our story

Contents

1

Prologue

Allison

MUCH OF THE TIME I think we go through life not realizing how good something is, but I was lucky. I knew.

My son, John, moved back to our hometown after college when he was 24. Gone was my fear that he'd die in some crazy antic, like capsizing a jon boat and getting caught in a riptide at 4 a.m., or end up in prison, or kill himself or someone else in a car accident. I no longer feared getting *that* phone call in the middle of the night.

On my deck on a steamy August afternoon, a massive oak canopying us, close family and friends gathered to celebrate John's graduation. He had left home after high school for two years before starting college basically on his own. He had chosen not "to walk," wanting only to come back to Greenville and start working. Like any special occasion at our old house, Flowers by Danny graced the dining room table with the scent of lilies wafting onto the deck. John was relaxed and happy, with his disarming smile, gentleness, quiet demeanor, and John F. Kennedy, Jr. looks. My daughter and her husband were up from Atlanta. I had a house again, I liked my job, and I was dating someone special. My life seemed to be settling back to something more like normal, nearly a decade after the divorce.

John had a job even though the recession was on and lived in a little apartment a few blocks from me. We checked in by phone every day, and once or twice a week we would meet for dinner. I could hear the happiness in my voice when I'd reject friends' offers to say, "I can't tonight; I'm meeting John!" I even had the awareness to say to him more than once, "I am so grateful for this time with you! I know it won't stay this way. You'll move away, get married, things will be different—but I really appreciate THIS time."

I frequently nagged him to get his hair cut, but he liked his long, rich, wavy locks. Although worried about money, overall he seemed happy getting started in his young-adult life.

In the twenty-five years I had worked in hospitals in various capacities, neither of my children had ever been interested in visiting me there. The second year that John was back in town, he called me twice to say he was coming to the hospital. The first time was for his paternal grandfather. I met John in the parking lot and went with him to the intensive care unit waiting room. It was John's first experience with that setting; his Pop-Pop died in the early-morning hours that September night. A lovely young resident named Kelli attended him throughout, checking in frequently with the family.

A few months later, John called me again to visit the hospital. A friend of his, a young man John's age, had been found unconscious downtown with a severe head injury. Again we met in the ICU waiting room. For the next several weeks, John's friends united through a website in support of Jeremy. Working then as a patient advocate, I visited regularly with the young man's mother as she made difficult decisions—finally, to take her son off life support. I was so aware—how one day he was here, laughing, and then he was not. *There but for the grace of God go I.* I didn't know how she could do it—go through this vigil with her beloved son. I marveled at her strength.

I met John on a cold, rainy day in late February, to sit with him and friends at Jeremy's funeral. When I walked into the crowded vestibule, at first I didn't recognize John. His hair was pulled back in a neat ponytail. In his black suit, he looked pale and gaunt. But it was a passing thought as we went into the somber celebration of a young man's life.

John

I've almost always lived within the range of ear-erecting blows of train whistles. Night trains that thundered down the tracks and take me still to memories of bedrooms past where I lay awake listening. To my grandparents' house in the mountains, where my grandfather would take my sister and me to a train crossing a couple of miles from their home to lay coins on the tracks, to be flattened by passing trains later in the day. Later Pop-Pop would make us breakfast with handpicked blueberries in our pancakes, throwing into the batter the occasional cotton ball as a prank. His red vibrating footrest was the coolest toy ever, and the dozens of keys hanging on the wall beside the garage door fascinated me. However, his genius idea of ridding his lawn of dandelions by giving all the cousins a penny for each one picked had backfired when we realized the neighbor's yard had a much better selection.

On Sundays we'd go to the church where he was pastor and squirm in the pews while he preached and our grandmother played the organ. When we were old enough, we'd be picked to be acolytes and envied by the rest of the cousins.

I guess I always thought my life was pretty good, even when my parents split up. I had my friends.

The morning I woke to a call telling me my friend, Jeremy, had been found unconscious downtown, I called my mom to tell her what was going on and to see if she could do anything to help his family. When you're unfamiliar with hospitals, it's a huge help to know someone who works there who can explain things and at least answer some of your questions.

I met my mom in the waiting room where his family and friends were camped out. Jeremy was put on a respirator via tracheostomy and, later, a feeding tube was inserted into his stomach. These procedures, known as being "trached and pegged," would keep him alive long enough for the swelling in his brain to subside. Even though he was young, strong, smart, handsome, and absolutely hilarious, Jeremy's body couldn't recover from the trauma, and his family had to make the decision to take him off life support. They also made the heroic decision to allow his perfect organs to be used to save the lives of multiple others.

Jeremy was my first friend to die. There had been several other tragic deaths of kids around my age in college, but none as close to me as this. We first met in high school when he was trying to take my girlfriend. Although he succeeded at that, I couldn't ever be mad at the guy. Later in high school we lived in the same apartment complex and then went to the same college.

I was sad and angry and confused. I was also friends with Jeremy's little brother, and I couldn't stop thinking about how it would affect their family. At some point after Jeremy died, I talked to my mom about it and told her I never wanted to be kept alive in that situation.

That thought came back to haunt me years later after I got out of the hospital, after being trached and pegged.

2

Wegener's

Allison—March, Year One

"THE BLUEROSE HAS THE absolute best scones," I said, putting a dab of butter on a last morsel. Tom nodded, his mouth full of fried eggs and corned beef hash.

We were seated outside the small café on a brilliant Saturday. Jasmine twined yellow around the trellis. I loved these weekend trips to Charleston, always one of my favorite places. Tom and I had begun dating seriously shortly before he was transferred there, so we'd done the commuter relationship for several months. I had also started a new position with my company just six weeks earlier, and disturbingly, my always healthy 26-year-old son had been having random bouts of sickness. But this morning was worry free as our comedienne waitress kept us laughing.

Then my son was calling.

"What? Yes, of course . . . . Let me know!" I said.

I hung up and met Tom's gaze, his startlingly blue eyes penetrating me.

"John is having bad stomach pain. He's going to urgent care and wanted to know if he could use my credit card to pay for it."

"What do you think is wrong?" Tom's question mirrored my concern.

"I just don't know, but he needs to see a real doctor! This is ridiculous! All these different symptoms! What could be wrong? Nobody's getting to the real problem, not since November."

"I could get my doctor to see him."

Tom still had a regular doctor in Greenville, whereas I only used my gynecologist and John hadn't had a doctor since he'd left the pediatrician.

"Sure, would you?" I asked, and Tom agreed to call her Monday morning.

"I need to go," I said, suddenly deciding to cut the weekend short. "Something's not right."

Soon I was on the road to Greenville, a box of scones on the seat beside me. As I drove, I called my daughter Megan to tell her this latest symptom. We talked about the randomness of his symptoms—at first flulike, then sinus problems and cough, now intense stomach pain? I hung up disturbed, and hopeful for the upcoming doctor's appointment.

Allison—April 13, Year One

My phone vibrating on the bedside table woke me from the escape of several hours' sleep.

"The pain is awful. I haven't been able to sleep at all. I waited 'til six to call. "

"Okay," I said, fully awake at the sound of John's voice and aware of a leaden dread. "I'm coming over. We've GOT to do something."

"Yeah."

As I hurriedly dressed, my mind re-ran a scenario of past days. The previous afternoon at the internal medicine doctor's office, the third time in three weeks for John, I had met him there and insisted that he be hospitalized. The doctor tried, but without a specific diagnosis, the hospital physician service said he would have to go through the emergency department. Knowing that the wait would be hours and in intense pain, this time with his shoulder, John refused. He left her office in a pained frenzy to go for a shoulder X-ray as I went to the pharmacy for yet another round of medications, this time strong painkillers. The wait at the pharmacy took forever, and all I could think about was how much he was hurting. He hadn't been able to eat anything and was almost pacing his apartment, the pain unrelieved, when I had left last night.

As I drove to his place, I didn't know what I would find when I got there or how I would manage, but I knew we were going to the hospital. My hospital. Two months ago I changed jobs, returning to the corporate marketing department and working contract at a small hospital about fifteen miles away. My administrator there was at a conference in D.C., but I called her anyway as I drove. She in turn called her colleague, the chief nursing officer, who was in an adjacent hotel room. By the time I got to John's, the Baptist Easley Emergency Department had been alerted that we were on the way. I told John, and this time he gave me little resistance. He was able to walk, and I got him into my car, headed for Easley.

John lay back in the seat, eyes closed. As I drove, my mind continued to try to make sense of the past weeks. John had always been so healthy. Except for ear infections prior to age five, he was hardly ever sick. But last November, he had a bad flu and never quite got well. All through January and February he complained—of sore throats, congestion, fatigue. In frustration, I said to him, too often, "You are never sick! What is wrong?! You've always been so healthy!"

One day he texted me at work to say he thought he had lupus. I told him emphatically that he did not and to get off the Internet.

Then the last Saturday in March, he again needed to go to urgent care—this time with severe stomach pain. And a few days later, Megan called me to say that John told her he'd been coughing up blood. *What was going on?*

Megan conferred with her medical-student friend Susan about the randomness of John's symptoms. "There really is a disease that has all those things," she said. "It's called Wegener's. But he wouldn't have *that*."

Tom's doctor had begun a series of lab tests on John. At a return visit a week later, he was dehydrated and anemic. The doctor tested him for every communicable disease, including AIDS. Then yesterday's visit had showed nothing conclusive other than a high rheumatoid factor and anemia, along with the shoulder pain.

Now, on Tuesday, April 13, we pulled up to the Baptist Easley emergency room. It was quiet at this early morning hour. They took us straight back, and as one nurse checked him, another got information from me and attempted to get his records from the doctor he'd seen.

Sensing that I had finally gotten him help, I momentarily leaned against the wall in the hallway, trembling. Someone brought me a cup of coffee and then took me to sit in a chair by John. A physician assistant came in to examine him, asking questions and ordering labs. The nurse manager told me they had called the hospitalist, a doctor who takes care of hospital inpatients; John would likely be admitted. She said his hemoglobin was 7. Normal was 12.

They started intravenous pain meds for him, and he began texting, his phone never to be far from his hand in the following weeks. I was getting texts on my own phone; one from my administrator in D.C. passing along the "official" word received there that John was "sick as stink." I texted Megan, who in turn contacted her father. John also told me that his girlfriend Anne, whom I had not met, was on her way from Charleston.

Soon the doctor came in. After thoroughly checking John and asking more questions, he said, "I think we are looking at Wegener's disease." *What Susan said*, I thought.

"What is that?" we both asked.

"Wegener's granulomatosis. It's an autoimmune disease that attacks the body's capillaries, causing them to hemorrhage. I want to run some more tests. We're going to admit you, John, and start you on steroids."

As the pain medication took effect and the staff worked with John to get him upstairs, I stepped out to call Megan and my ex-husband Vic. I had a diagnosis to give them and to tell them that John was being admitted. They had already started driving, Megan from Atlanta and Vic and his wife, Janet, from North Carolina. Two of my co-workers had heard we were here and had come to find me. I didn't feel quite as scared, knowing John and I weren't alone now; we had a tentative diagnosis, and something was being done for him.

A few hours later, the five of us who were to become John's care team in ensuing months convened in his room. John was being given nasal oxygen and seemed to be feeling better. Anne, a lovely lithe blonde, stood in the corner by the head of his bed. Vic and Janet, Megan and I, all gathered around. That it was an unusual gathering would not have been perceptible to onlookers. We didn't know Anne, and our family relationships had been strained since the divorce. Yet we all rallied around John, waiting to learn more, to know what was next.

Soon the doctor came back to the room to talk with us all. He further explained the disease. It was not curable but could go into remission with steroids and chemotherapy. It had no known cause. Wegener's was very rare, he said; only one in 30,000-50,000 people had it. It was considered an autoimmune disease, meaning that the body's immune system attacks its own tissue.

The doctor said, "You should feel better after a couple of weeks on the steroids."

Then he abruptly added, "The last case of Wegener's I had, the patient decided to take the meth (methamphetamines) route and was dead in four months."

In the second of shocked silence, John muttered, "Well, I'm not going to do THAT."

I thought the doctor was callous to even say such a thing. Of course John was going to be fine!

The next forty-eight hours blurred. With others there for John and new in my job, I kept trying to work, checking in on him periodically. But the afternoon of the second day, I was called to his room when the doctor was there. John's breathing was worse and he needed to be transferred to Greenville, to the trauma hospital's intensive care unit. As I was absorbing this, a nurse-friend took me aside to make sure I understood what the doctor was saying. When he got to Greenville, they would likely intubate him.

"You mean he would be unconscious?" I faltered, visualizing the tube that would be down his throat and the machine helping him to breathe. I motioned for his father to come over. My friend explained why—that John's lungs needed to rest and the ventilator would breathe for him. Trembling, I waited with the rest of the "team" in John's room for the ambulance attendants to strap him onto a stretcher. We followed in separate cars, my heart in deep fear, my mind still struggling to comprehend the magnitude of what was happening. I called my cousin Elaine in Atlanta to tell her the latest.

"I don't know what's happening," I said. "I don't know what to do." Calls like this one to her and to her sister Diane in Florida would become steady.

John—How it all started

At first I just thought it was the flu. It was the fall of 2009 and the swine flu was a big scare. My symptoms were similar to flu I'd known, but worse, so I assumed the "swine" part was what was getting me. It had been years since I had been to a doctor.

After high school I lived in Charleston for a couple of years until starting the University of South Carolina in 2004. Like my dad and unlike my mom and sister, I was rarely sick. Growing up, my need for doctors and hospitals was limited to ear tubes and yearly check-ups, so going six or so years without insurance was a non-issue. Thankfully, I bought insurance through the small manufacturing company I was working for before I became ill. I almost switched it for something less expensive just months earlier. But my deductible was high, and being 26 and on the verge of poverty, I spent several months going to "doc-in-a-box" outfits. I guess you get what you pay for in that regard. None of them took me seriously. If you complain of pain in those places they roll their eyes, write an antibiotic prescription, and hand you a bill.

After months of being treated like a junkie and continually getting worse, I broke down and went to what I thought was a legitimate private practice family doc. Weeks went by with that office calling me to come in to get blood tests for a dozen deadly diseases, some of which I had heard of and many that I had to look up. These initial blood draws were the beginning of a long relationship with nurses with needles.

The visits were tough because of the waiting period between having the blood drawn and getting the results back. At one point they told me they were going to test for HIV/AIDS. I called my dad as soon as I left the doctor's office to tell him. It was a turning point in the whole process.

Don't know about you, but my family didn't exactly discuss sexual relationships over dinner. The fact that I was telling him made everything that much more real. Luckily, my dad (having been a chaplain and counselor to students at a local college) was possibly the easiest person to talk to on the planet. My chance of having AIDS was slim to none, but it felt more like 90 percent during the two weeks it took to get the results back. After so many months and so many tests, my brain was allowing ANYTHING to be the answer. Was it AIDS? How in the hell could I have gotten AIDS? Is it even possible? Well, yeah idiot, it's gotta be possible. Maybe it's cancer. Maybe it's from smoking cigarettes or drinking beer or picking on some kid in middle school. Maybe I don't talk to my family enough or work hard enough or believe in God enough. When was the last time I went to church?! I wonder if there's mold in my apartment? Are there chemicals at work? How do I even ask anyone that? Shit. I'm probably missing too much work. My account is behind and it's gonna be my ass!

For the most part I knew these things weren't the problem. Not being able to figure out the problem is an awful feeling, and a feeling common to people with autoimmune diseases. It was scary and painful.

My joints were hurting so badly I could barely sleep; I was having to contort my body any way I could to relieve the pain. My throat had white ulcers the size of dimes, I was going on two months of one or more respiratory infections, and I was having ear infections for the first time since I had tubes removed at age five. Other than minor surgery placing and removing tubes four separate times before elementary school years, I'd had consistently good health. I had stitches in my knee once (from running into a bench while checking out the girls' soccer team), a broken toe or finger here and there, and a dislocated shoulder. That was it.

After weeks of going to work in the morning, coming home during lunch to pass out, returning to work for a few hours and then straight home after work to try to get some sleep, I agreed to let my mom pick me up from my apartment and take me to the ER. She drove me straight to the hospital where she worked, knowing it would have the shortest wait. I can't remember what I was thinking at that point. The pain had been constant for weeks, I was down ten or fifteen pounds, I had been coughing up blood, and I hadn't had a full night's sleep in longer than I could remember. I guess I called my on-again-off-again, long-distance girlfriend before I got to the hospital, but I don't remember that anymore either. And I'm sure my mom was scared to death.

I wasn't in the best shape of my life, but I was jogging and lifting weights several times a week. My diet had always been fairly healthy. I drank alcohol and smoked cigarettes from time to time and experimented with drugs in high school and college. My family history included some heart trouble and Alzheimer's, but nothing out of the ordinary.

These were all things I talked about with the doctors and in front of my family. Although my family loved me unconditionally, they had no false pretenses of my sainthood. Already I knew any information I could give might help.

Allison—April 15, Year One

At Greenville's intensive care unit, they did not intubate him—at least not then. When we got back to see him, he was in the cubicle right next to the one where his Pop-Pop had been. John, still alert, recognized it, too. It seemed surreal that this time it was John in the ICU, not Pop-Pop, or Jeremy. I thought about Jeremy's mother, how I had so empathized with her and wondered how she had withstood what she had to bear.

We met the ICU doctor and his senior resident who told us they would do a bronchoscopy, a procedure to look into John's lungs, within the next few hours. They were also scheduling a kidney biopsy for the next day; biopsy was the only definitive way to diagnose Wegener's. The young resident, Kelli, who was so helpful during Pop-Pop's term in the ICU recognized us and came to check, concerned. I felt as if we had a friend and ally in the vastness of the university hospital's maze. It was a place I frequented often in my previous job as a patient advocate, but never had my only son been there in a bed.

Back in the waiting room, friends began to call and converge, hearing the news by text and Facebook. We discussed starting a CarePages journal, as his friend's family had done, but John didn't want us to. "Mom, you know we can't do *that*." He knew I would know what he meant. He didn't want to put his friends through another experience like Jeremy's.

A couple of days later, after the kidney biopsy and the confirmation of Wegener's, John, still on nasal oxygen, went to a regular room on the pulmonary floor. He was getting blood transfusions and doctors started him on oral Cytoxan, the recommended chemotherapy treatment for Wegener's. They informed us of the side effects—susceptibility to cancers, possible infertility. Friends came to visit, and John was asking to go home. But his breathing continued to worsen, with his "sats," measure of oxygen saturation, decreasing.

Then a new pulmonologist came in to say that John's case was coming on "very aggressively," and that he needed to be on a massive steroid dosage and plasmapheresis, a process of washing the blood. She was very forceful and painted a dire picture. John reacted negatively, and we all felt this doctor lacked a good bedside manner. John was reassured when the rheumatologist came in that weekend and said he was on the right treatment and should stay the course. We all breathed again.

But our resident-friend, Kelli, cautioned me, saying, "The pulmonologist is really good. She told the residents that if we couldn't get excited about this young man, then we didn't need to be doctors." At the time, we didn't realize how right this doctor was, and that she would become a trusted resource in Greenville in ensuing months.

Doctors, trying to determine a cause, kept asking us about any possible heredity factors. We searched our brains and came up with nothing. I tried to think why this could be happening. The only thought that kept running through my head was the scripture verse about the "sins of the fathers (or mothers)," when the Pharisees questioned Jesus about the man blind from birth. No parent wants to be the reason, even unintentionally through genetics, for a child's illness. I heard only the response Jesus gave to their question: "that the Son of Man might be glorified." I prayed that God's will might be manifested in this situation.

John—April 15, Year One

The first bit of luck I had seen in a long time came shortly after arriving at Baptist Easley. I was tentatively diagnosed by a doctor who had seen Wegener's once before. It was such a strange sensation to know what it was—a mixture of relief, fear, uncertainty, and hope. I had been tested for more diseases, disorders, and illnesses than I knew existed.

My then-girlfriend, Anne, dropped everything she was doing (which was preparing for grad school finals) to drive from Charleston to Greenville. She met my entire family for the first time that day (they not having a clue I had a girlfriend at all) and worked out a way to stay by my side almost every day for the next year.

At some point the first IV was put in so that I could be given some pain meds. It took a lot more pain medication than the staff expected before I felt able to relax enough to pull my arm down from over my head where I had been holding it for the last day or so. Painless, dreamless sleep finally came. From this point on, my sense of time and understanding of events outside of my hospital room would become unclear.

Allison—April/May, Year One

On a Sunday, Megan, Anne, and I went to clean John's apartment that he shared with two roommates (one of whom was a neuro-trauma nurse who happened to be present when he was first intubated). Since John kept talking about going home, or maybe we just needed to do something we could, we went to prepare his place. While the girls worked in his room, stripping the bed, doing laundry, getting his clothes together, I cleaned his bathroom. Looking at all the various bottles of prescription and over-the-counter medications by his sink collected over the past months, I felt every symptom he had told me about—the sinus congestion, cough, sore throat, horrible ulcers inside his mouth and throat, stomach pain, terrible joint and muscle pain, fever and chills, extreme fatigue. *I didn't know how sick he was, I didn't know what else to do, I am so sorry.* These thoughts cried out in every part of my being as I scrubbed.

Anne left the next day to go back to Charleston, her graduate school program, and her part-time job. She had been with us for almost a week, staying with John every night, and we had come to love her. Vic and Janet had gone back to North Carolina. Megan had stayed with me and started to look for a better place for John to live. We all knew he couldn't manage the singles' lifestyle in a high-rise downtown apartment complex any more.

I was at the hospital with John, early and late, working some in between. Friends started funds for us, one at Baptist Easley Hospital and another at First Baptist Church Greenville, and brought him food and movies and books. John kept us all focused with his own positive attitude and insistence on getting out of the hospital. His friends began a blood drive for him.

But again within a couple of days, he was in trouble.

Megan went to John's room that morning and noticed he was pale. Then he was coughing, and she saw blood in his hand and on his T-shirt. She got the nurse, and soon respiratory therapists were in the room with a portable breathing machine and an apparatus for his face. She called me; even the oxygen facemask was not enough. I got to his room just as he was rushed back to ICU.

We were told to go to the ICU waiting room. Within minutes, a doctor came to get me, explaining that John needed to be intubated and they needed for me to sign permission. Shaking, I walked with Megan into the ICU. This time it felt like a dream. I walked automatically, aware of people-shapes around me with voices that seemed muffled. Then, standing at the foot of John's cubicle, I could barely see him as nurses and techs worked on him. I signed for the intubation, thinking, *He doesn't have a Living Will; what if he wouldn't want this . . . .* Then some doctor, with an accent so heavy I could not understand him, thrust a clipboard at me to sign for another procedure.

"An incision," he was saying. "In his groin. In the artery."

"What? Why? What is it for?" I asked.

His hurry came across as anger as he tried to explain. Everyone else was too busy around John to listen or to ask. I thought it was for a catheter to start the plasmapheresis process; it didn't seem to matter whether I understood. I signed permission, sensing that this really was not a question, not a choice. Then there were more papers to sign, for units of blood to be transfused, and we were escorted out.

Once more, Vic and Janet and Anne hurried back to Greenville, and we all convened in the ICU waiting room. No more than two people at a time could go back and only at specific times, and not even then if John was having a procedure. We claimed a section of the waiting room and talked or rested as we could.

John had so many specialists and they didn't always agree on what should be done, so it was very difficult to get any clear communication about what was happening. As one friend said about his experience with his patient, "There's no quarterback." Finally I asked for a conference to be arranged. We all gathered in the small conference room off the ICU waiting room, where they put you when they have bad news, and waited for several doctors.

The nephrologists were worried about his kidneys and how the Cytoxan and other drugs would affect them. The rheumatologist had delayed, thinking that the more conservative dosing would be enough. Only the pulmonologist had pushed for more aggressive treatment. We learned that day that "lungs trump kidneys," and that Pulmonology would be calling the shots. Good to know.

The second day, Megan, with approval from the rest of us, decided to override John's wishes and start his story on CarePages. On Apr 22, 2010, 5:37p.m., she began:

> John has been hospitalized since last Tuesday, April 13. Through multiple blood tests and organ biopsies, his doctors have diagnosed his condition as Wegener's disease. We are grateful to all of you who have been tracking his progress through calls, email, texts, and visits to the hospital. Now that John is back in the ICU and unable to connect with you directly, we have decided to expand our email chain to this site so everyone can stay as informed as they would like to be!
>
> John is currently on his second stay in the Greenville ICU. Over the weekend his condition seemed to be improving and we were even hopeful he might go home, but early yesterday morning his breathing worsened and his doctors—a team comprised of pulmonologists (lung), nephrologists (kidney), and rheumatologists (no good common word for that one) decided to begin treating him more aggressively. He has been put on a ventilator, which is doing his breathing for him and giving his lungs a rest for a couple days. Yesterday he had a round of plasmapheresis, which allows the doctors to actually remove the toxins from his blood and return it to his body. It went well and he is scheduled to do it again a few times over the next week or so. The Wegener's is causing his lungs to bleed, but the doctor reported this morning that the alveolar hemorrhaging has slowed significantly and therefore his hemoglobin has returned to a point that allows them to continue treating him with a form of chemo which, combined with steroids, should help put the disease in remission. John has had a quiet day today and we are thankful for that. I will start updating this page with any news we hear, so please

forward the link to anyone you know who would like to keep up with John's progress.

Love, Megan Greene Roberts

The entries we made of John's situation went out to hundreds of supporters. For months, CarePages became a lifeline for me with messages and assurances of prayer from friends, family, and loved ones, many of whom I had never met.

During visiting hours the second night in ICU, I noticed that besides the ventilator and all the tubes going in and out of John, the drainage bag from his kidneys was bright red. I called it to the nurse's attention and she just nodded. I didn't need to be a medical professional to know this was not good. Driving out of the parking lot an hour later, I called my cousin Diane and choked out, "I don't think he's going to make it." All the evidence showed that John was continuing to bleed out his very life-blood, and there was nothing more to do but keep transfusing and waiting.

I didn't get a call in the night and John kept fighting, now getting the Cytoxan intravenously. The bleeding in his lungs was better. On Saturday, he was moved from ICU to the Coronary Care Unit, because they had more room there. We liked CCU much better. Instead of curtained cubicles, the rooms had glass doors and windows and were larger. More than two of us could be with him. The waiting room, too, was larger, quieter, and less crowded. John, still intubated and necessarily heavily sedated, didn't know where he was. But I fully believed that he knew we were there. I was so grateful that all his family was around him and prayed that would be healing for him.

By Sunday the word was out about John, and extended family and friends, many whom I hadn't seen since the divorce, filled the CCU waiting room. I was somewhat surprised. Divorce, at least in this town, was isolating. But longtime couple-friends showed up bearing cups of Starbucks and concern. The braver of John's friends came, some with their parents. Most followed on the CarePages network.

Tom brought his mother, my dear friend Elizabeth, from Columbia. She had become like a mother to me, and John had told his friends that she was like his grandmother. I took her back to see John. Tall and slender, beautifully statuesque with silver hair, she looked like an angel as she stood by his bed, praying for him. It was all we could do.

For the next while, all we had to go on were the clinical details shared with us—readings from X-rays, and numbers, lots of numbers. Hemoglobin, white cells, creatinine. As John's lungs would improve, his kidney function would decline. We held onto these details, these numbers; they were all we had as John lay mostly still with the machine breathing for him. Sometimes he was restless; it was hard to keep him sedated enough, and more sedation had to be added as the days on the ventilator increased.

At work, there was a crisis with the new brand/logo, and I was called on spur of the moment to present to the board of directors. Years of training paid off and I managed to do a professional performance; the situation was resolved. My mind was elsewhere, though, focused on John's situation. I felt angry that I had to go through the performance of my job when my heart was at the bedside with John. But not working was not an option. My job was my only source of income, and any savings had been long gone.

Within about another week, John's white cell count started to come down some, which meant the chemo was working. Doctors began decreasing the ventilator support and also lowering the sedation. For the first time in three weeks, I felt something other than shock and fear. I think it was hope.

Then doctors told us they might extubate the next day. I had to manage a major photo shoot that was scheduled to take pictures throughout the hospital for a new website. I was in charge and needed to be there. I alerted my two coworkers in Easley that I would have to leave if doctors decided to take John off the ventilator.

Holding my phone close, hating that I was not with John, I watched for Megan's text. We were in the cath lab when I got the word: they were going to extubate. I ran out, making it to the Greenville hospital in twenty minutes.

I got to John's room and it was over. Reportedly, it was uneventful. The doctor tugged and John coughed. John, however, was upset—tearful and disturbed. He tried to punch his father and swung at the nurses. He was okay having me nearby. He was given Ativan, and his agitation and confusion worsened. He was still getting massive doses of steroids, one gram a day, was still on oxygen, and still had a naso-gastric (NG) tube in his nose for feedings. That afternoon, he also had a PICC line surgically placed subclavian, under his collarbone area, so that medications could be given there as well as in his arms.

That night's nurse was very intolerant of us and dismissed us at 10. I left wondering if I should have stayed, regardless. I went to bed, trusting him to God's care, to do for him what I could not.

The next morning, Saturday, May 1, John had an infection, fever, and some delirium. At 5 p.m., they took him for a head CT; he was having right-sided weakness, tremors, and altered mental status. They changed his NG tube to a smaller one and removed the oxygen, trying to make him more comfortable. He was still so sick.

My CarePages entry that day was, *The past three weeks have been "walking through the valley of the shadow . . . ." Thank you for all your loving thoughts and prayers; I have felt them and been upheld by them.*

And later that night, he seemed better. He was more coherent and responded, "I love you, too." Again, we all left him that night. The next day, physical, occupational, and speech therapies were ordered. His numbers kept fluctuating. He was still trying to get up. And that night, the infection and fever worsened.

Will this onslaught never stop? I agonized. Every time we thought he was getting better, something else happened. We were in the fourth week now.

I realized later that during this time, he was suffering from withdrawal from all the heavy sedation he'd been given while intubated. He had vivid monstrous nightmares; he would rise up out of bed and tell Megan fiercely that they had to *get out, now,* that horrible creatures were after them. He talked repeatedly about having to get off the train. Nurses said, "We see this a lot with the young people; it takes so much to keep them down and then it's so hard to come off of."

It was horrible to watch. At times he had to be restrained, for his safety. He slept and I stayed with him until his father came at 9 p.m. Vic stayed with him a couple of nights, to try to keep him on the bed. One night John ripped out his NG tube. We didn't let friends back during these days and kept the CarePages postings fairly neutral. Megan or Anne or both stayed with him most of every day.

When I got home that night, my friend Libba had brought supper. Megan and Anne were already eating, sitting on the living room sofa. I joined them and felt like I had a family again after too many years of aloneness.

John—May, Year One

The first few weeks felt hopeless. Although it was nice to finally have a name for the disease I was suffering from, that name brought with it fear. I remember looking up Wegener's granulomatosis online and seeing a life expectancy of four months before someone figured out that steroids helped immensely.

It's amazing how easily the brain can forget pain and anguish. When I think back at the times I was in the most pain, when I wondered if the pain itself could actually kill me, I can't remember the actual physical pain but only my mind telling me *something has to change soon or you're going to die.* Maybe it's a defense mechanism the body and brain use to keep themselves going. There were several times I told myself I couldn't go through it again, no matter what. That I would rather die than have that same procedure or mix of drugs again.

It was like that coming off of extreme sedatives after being unconscious for a few days. It's like trying to describe a dream, in this case a nightmare. There were three main parts to my return to consciousness. The first was the most frightening. My semiconscious mind pulled at bits of information in my immediate surroundings and processed them in my Versed- and fear-soaked brain. The result was torture, torment, and a general idea of Hell.

In the first "dream" I was trapped in a couple's house. I didn't know them but I knew they were doctors and friends of a doctor I knew. I was tied up in their home (actually restrained in my hospital bed) and no one would give me water (happening in real life because of procedures and tests.) After what felt like weeks of this, a team of men with guns came to the house to kill me. I specifically remember shooting two men while I was crouching behind a couch. In reality I even asked my sister to get rid of the gun I thought I used to kill them, which I thought was under the sheets in my hospital bed. Later, while closer to consciousness, besides thinking I was married, I believed that I had killed people and police would be there to arrest me at any minute.

The second dream was set in an old train/subway car. There were several of us who seemed to be on the train for eternity, while others seemed to get off at stops. The characters in this play included an old wise man to my right, two wraiths who came and went usually together (Megan and Anne), and an indescribable life form in front of me. I don't remember much of the full dream other than being alone and scared in a large house of glass and concrete with white foamy waves crashing all around.

I can imagine how unbelievable and, frankly, silly these "dreams" sound. There will never be a way for me to convey how real and terrifying they were. More real at the time than life itself.

Allison—May, Year One

May 4 was a big day—John passed the swallow study and held a juice cup by himself! Lab results showed that the infection was better. And that night he got his first "formed" food—a pork chop, corn, and mashed potatoes. It looked like something from a Play Dough Factory; the pureed pork shaped into a chop, the corn into an ear. John smiled with disgust; Megan took a picture and put it on CarePages. It was good to have something to laugh about. The doctors kept telling us he was "on the up and up," and we kept asking them to repeat it, just to hear the good news again.

John worked hard to get back the basics of life—swallowing, eating, talking, standing, sitting. I watched as he tried to feed himself, struggling for the hand-to-eye coordination to get food onto a spoon and then navigate it to his mouth. This was my tall, healthy son who played four varsity sports. His front teeth had been chipped during the rush to intubate him, and his voice was a hoarse whisper. But soon he was sitting up in a chair and walking, with help, around the room. The inpatient rehab hospital was evaluating him daily to see if he would be a fit to go there for several weeks. He had a wonderful nurse during this time, Scott, who wasn't much older than John and treated him like a brother.

Anne was leaving that Friday for her graduation back in Charleston, having written her final exam sitting in CCU. The evening before she left, John told her about his stepmother's offer. Janet had offered their extra house, unrented and across the street from them, in their small North Carolina town. John, and Anne if she wished, could go and stay there and maybe find a job there later. I was quiet; this was the first I had heard of this plan. As he was telling Anne, John was watching me. He finally said to Anne, "Look at her face."

Anne turned to me and asked, "What?"

I said only, "I would miss you very much."

John and I had been so close the past years. To think of him being a few hours away was hard. While Megan had left town after high school graduation and never looked back, John and I both thought Charleston was the only possible place better than Greenville to ever live. But I knew that I didn't have the resources to offer more. I had a tiny two-bedroom, one-bathroom house, and I had to be at work all the time. Anne was non-committal, but I could tell John was relieved and grateful to have this plan.

John's best friend since childhood, who'd been traveling on the other side of the world, returned and came to visit. Smith sat by the head of the bed and John leaned in to him, eyes closed and a relaxed smile on his face. I couldn't help but notice the stark contrast of the two "brothers"—one darkly tanned and fit, the other bloated and pasty-white with thinning hair. My heart twisted.

The following Sunday, May 9, was Mother's Day. John, still in CCU, enjoyed a shower and was waiting for possible transfer to the rehab hospital the next day. We celebrated Mother's Day with a picnic on his bed. With Megan and her husband Haynes, and John and Anne, it was a wonderful time.

That afternoon we learned that John was suddenly being transferred to a non-intensive care room in the hospital. He sat in a chair as we gathered things from the room he'd been in for two weeks. It was about four o'clock when he began complaining of a pain in his upper right thigh and another in his left calf. The doctor ordered a doppler study, a type of ultrasound. He was still swollen from the excessive amounts of steroids and his compromised kidney function. Early evening he was transferred to a room on the pulmonary floor; by that time the lower part of his body was swollen to bursting. His weight, from steroids and fluid retention, peaked at 235.

Monday we got the confirmation of blood clots, one in each leg, and also that John would not be going to the rehab hospital. We learned that he had a heparin reaction (HIT), which caused the clots. He would have to be on a blood thinner, Coumaden. His kidneys were in trouble, and nephrologists followed him closely as he worked to be able to go home or to rehab. He was transferred again, this time to a room on the cancer unit to better accommodate his need for plasmapheresis and chemotherapy infusion. His legs had to be wrapped because the intense swelling was causing the skin to literally split, and he was in much pain. We had gone to K-Mart to buy extra-large sweats and T-shirts to accommodate his expanded size.

We went through these moves, these machinations, almost by rote, thinking each time that he would get better, that this latest complication, bad news, *couldn't* be happening. Every time he seemed to be better, something else slapped him down. It was all too desperate to process; we could only react to the next crisis.

Still, John and one or both of the girls watched TV, movies and cooking shows and tried to function as normally as possible. The notebook we kept in the room had entries from all of us: lists of foods he could not eat while on Coumadin and with the steroid-induced diabetes he now had; instructions from various doctors on their multiple rounds along with notations of his vital signs; a take-out dinner order for me to pick up; sketches of possible tattoo designs he wanted; someone's wish list: San Francisco and Northern California, New Orleans, Chicago, Harry Potter World, Vegas/ Garth Brooks, St. Croix.

A few days later, we enjoyed a picnic in front of the hospital, with food brought from the local Greek Festival. Despite the pain in his lower extremities and in a wheel chair, mandatory IV pole linked to his arm, John was witty, intuitive, and abreast of more details than the rest of us could fathom.

Discharge plans were underway with a target of Friday, May 21. Nephrologists were confident in the stability of his kidney numbers, he was back on oral Cytoxan and steroids, his INR would have to be checked regularly with the Coumaden, he would be on home insulin and have to manage his steroid-induced diabetes. He would keep his Greenville doctors during his acute recovery before transferring to others in Asheville (the necessary physicians closest to Franklin); staff was working on coordinating outpatient appointments for him. But he would finally be leaving the hospital and going home—to his dad's and Janet's. I hadn't taken time to process that.

Then the following day, he was having chest pain, his hemoglobin was dropping, and he was coughing up blood and getting more transfusions. He couldn't walk or sit in a chair anymore. An ophthalmologist was called in to check a problem with his eyes, another manifestation of the Wegener's. Challenging conversations with doctors began again, and we felt like we were getting no answers. No one seemed to know what to do. He was definitely getting worse instead of better.

All of us were scared. That weekend, we cleared out John's apartment, putting his things into storage. I began the actions of applying for disability insurance for him.

On May 26, a Thursday, we were all in John's room. Megan had come back from Atlanta the night before, and Vic and Janet had come that day, too, to join Anne and me. I knew he needed to be transferred elsewhere, after nearly seven weeks here. We had consulted with his doctors; John's case was more complicated than they were used to. It's hard for doctors to admit that.

My seven years of experience as a patient advocate had taught me not to be intimidated by doctors, and I was familiar with hospital procedures. I requested a transfer. Vic was doing Internet research. Recommendations were the Mayo Clinic, Johns Hopkins, or Duke. I opted for Duke, the closest, knowing I would not be able to afford to get there otherwise. The decision was cinched when Vic's sister-in-law found that a pre-eminent specialist in Wegener's was at Duke. Dr. Nancy Allen returned Vic's call and agreed to take John's case. John's pulmonologist worked with Duke's critical care team to get him admitted to the medical intensive care unit (MICU). By 4 p.m., we knew that he would be transferred by ambulance to Duke University Medical Center that evening. It all happened at such amazing speed, after weeks of waiting. Fortunately at this point, John was still stable enough to be moved.

I was at the breakpoint of exhaustion. I would come to feel this way so many times that it would become repetitively, uselessly boring, and pointless even to acknowledge. This time the girls, Anne and Megan, looked at each other and agreed that they would be the ones to go up initially with him that night. Megan was a self-employed artist; Anne had quit her job in Charleston, after finishing her graduate program, to be with John. Anne remembered that her father's first cousin lived in Durham and was a nurse at Duke. She called this cousin, Cathy, and asked if they could stay with her. (As it happened, this cousin was the charge nurse in the MICU where John was going!) Neither the girls nor I knew anything about Durham.

Ambulance attendees came into John's room at 8 p.m. and strapped him on a gurney for a nearly five-hour ride. We all hugged him goodbye. I knew he was terrified and didn't want to go alone. The girls left behind him, promising to see him at Duke around 1a.m. Vic and Janet went back to their home in Franklin, planning to go to Duke the following day. I went home to collapse and then try to work, my first days away from John since the initial hospitalization on April 13.

Those seven weeks in Greenville were dulled in my memory, rather like sleepwalking underwater. Because the others—Anne, Megan, Vic and

Janet—were often present and because I was so desperately trying to keep working, I was in-and-out of John's immediate care and more intent on managing it. That was the only way I knew how to do it.

Duke would be a different story.

John—May 26, Year One

Cytoxan is standard procedure for Wegener's patients and has saved many lives. I'm sure those who are alive because of it are grateful and glad to have had it. I am not one of those people.

The word itself sounds "toxic" for a reason; it is. Before it was administered to me, there was an especially annoying medical student who insisted on telling me every few minutes that once it was used on me, I'd be sterile. He must've come to my bedside five times. I can appreciate his eagerness to make me aware of the life-changing side effects of this particular drug, for they are many and severe. But after confirming with docs that Cytoxan was my only option at the time, hearing possible side effects more than once was just depressing. Other possible side effects for Cytoxan (generically known as cyclophosphamide) are liver failure, kidney and urinary tract problems, heart and lung problems, secondary cancers, swelling, blistering, peeling, bleeding, and every other horrible thing one can think of.

I definitely cried that night. Throughout my time in the hospital, I continuously adjusted my vision of what I had previously assumed would be a pretty normal life. Possibly not having kids wasn't a small change.

So—Wegener's sucks. It may have taken the first two months of my hospitalization before I even got the name right. Wegener's granulomatosis. As in, Dr. Wegener discovered this wonderful autoimmune disease that, to my understanding, attacks your body's organs by causing inflammation of the blood vessels and producing granulomas that destroy normal tissue. Because Dr. Wegener was a Nazi, the name of the disease has been officially changed to Granulomatosis with Polyangiitis. Since it took my asking doctors, nurses, and family members to repeat, spell, and sound out Wegener's granulomatosis over several weeks so I could learn it, I'll be damned if I give it all up a few years later. So I'll just call it Wegener's. Besides, it's brutal, deadly, and threateningly mysterious, so a Nazi's name seems somewhat fitting.

Allison—June, Year One

John had been at Duke for more than a week. He had an IVC filter placed, to keep the blood clots from moving upward, and another femoral catheter inserted for plasmapheresis; that procedure had been excruciating for him.

That first weekend alone in Greenville, exhausted and still stunned, I hid in the cocoon of my bed and cried for my mother. At this point in my life, she had been dead for 18 years and I had gone through a divorce, moves, near-poverty, graduations, Megan's wedding, and a couple of relationships without her. Yet now I cried. I cried for her, too, for how sad she would have been that this terrible thing was happening to our John. I was glad that she did not have to bear it.

I was an only child, born late in my parents' lives. My father died when I was 30, three weeks after John was born; my mother died when I was 38. Up until the last few years of her death at age 85, my mother was the strongest person in my life. While I was trying to run a business and a home and finish graduate school, my mother kept John several days a week after preschool. A teacher for 35 years, she adored her two grandchildren. Until the time of her heart attack at 82, consequent failing health and ensuing dementia, she cooked for the four of us every Sunday and on occasional weeknights. Her death, too early in my life, nevertheless allowed us to have a better-than-we-could afford house and lifestyle for a time.

She used to tell me frequently, "He is so smart!" but she didn't like it when he was rough with his sister or too "rambunctious." John was "all boy," as his first babysitter always said. His first toy was a ball, and he was adept at handling virtually every kind in his sports-filled life.

Now he was lying in another hospital bed in a strange city at the age of 26.

John—ICU, June, Year One

Lying in the ICU, I heard someone's screams. He must've been terrified. I knew he was in pain, but I didn't think he would've been screaming like that just from pain. He couldn't have been more than three or four "rooms" to my right. Rooms in the ICU were curtained on three sides with a wall at the back, so sound traveled.

There were occasional moans and screams of pain in the ICU, but mostly the sounds of machines keeping those poor souls alive. Although some of their "souls" may have been long gone.

Nighttime was the worst, dark and lonely. I had actually gotten two or three hours of sleep on the night he came in. I don't remember for sure, but I think he woke me up. Doctors' and nurses' voices were frantic and trying to give direction in a volume above his screams, though I couldn't tell what they were saying. I remembered him screaming cusses as loud as he could, and I couldn't help but put his story together in my head.

He sounded young. Probably a local high school or Duke student. Being only a couple of years out of college myself, I began thinking of my friends back home and hoping they were all safe.

For some God-awful reason, there was a clock on the wall right in front of me. I spent some nights watching the second hand and counting the ticks until morning brought visiting hours and a feeling of safety with my family there that allowed me to sleep. When I checked it this night, it was about 3 a.m., so I figured he probably got in a wreck while going home from a bar. My mind pictured him a few beds over with doctors and nurses crowded around him on all sides to repair some kind of major injury. For some reason, I was picturing him losing a leg. He would scream for a while and pass out. It was a relief for me, and I assumed for those working on him, when he was quiet. He was eventually taken to surgery (I guessed), and I fell back asleep.

Sometime later, I was awakened to his screams after he returned. This time I didn't hear any hospital staff with him. Just his screaming through the pain and fear.

I knew pain by this point. It took months before I was diagnosed with Wegener's granulomatosis, an incredibly painful disease. Other than the disease itself, I had been through at least a dozen procedures, some with no anesthesia and many done by students, possibly for their first time. Extreme pain with a clear head I usually endured with a clenched jaw and near silence. The dreamy haze of unconsciousness that comes with large amounts of painkillers and sedatives is what brought out my screams of terror; I believe the technical term is ICU psychosis. Although still in pain while on these, it's the nightmares in my head that set them off. A painful procedure that lasts thirty minutes can be turned into a weeklong torture session with intent to kill by the mind on drugs.

That night I sat in my bed, at this point attached to oxygen and all kinds of tubes, and prayed for both of us. I had been in the hospital at least two months. I'm not exactly sure because it was almost impossible for me to differentiate days, other than what hospital and what unit and condition I was in. I knew I was at Duke in the ICU and with a breathing apparatus, so it was anywhere between two and four months.

He stopped screaming sometime before morning, and there was a short hustle and bustle before all was quiet in the unit, other than the usual sound of machines pumping life and false hope into the bodies around me. Whoever he was and whatever happened to him, I knew he wasn't alive when the sun came up.

Many possibilities of my future had gone through my mind up to this point. How would I live with this disease? Would I have to live with my parents? What quality of life would I have? Would I be able to have children? Would I be able to provide for myself? Would I be permanently disabled? Would anyone want to marry me? These were all valid questions with impossible answers, but after listening to this young man die, I realized that none of that mattered. It was the first time I thought about dying. Maybe I had thought some about it before, but not to the extent of how much I would scream, how bad it would hurt, and how terrible it would be to die alone and in pain.

Allison—June, Year One

I left for Duke the following Saturday with Tom driving me up. I had always been afraid to drive any distance alone and could hardly see at all at night. I didn't even want to have a car in a strange city; I would walk where I needed to go. We were delayed leaving and had to stop along the way, and I was frustrated that it was taking so long. Megan called to say that again John was having trouble breathing, the bleeding was worse, and he was being taken back to intensive care. We didn't get there until a few minutes after 2 p.m.; the visiting period had just ended. The girls filled us in and decided to stay another night to see how he did.

We soon learned that he had a "yeast infection in his blood." That doesn't sound too bad, I thought.

Vic and Janet arrived on Wednesday, after John could barely breathe Tuesday afternoon. The yeast infection was cryptoccocus, something actually very bad. Infectious disease specialists were called in. Vic and I stood on opposite sides of John's bed. John reached for my hand and then Vic's. United through him, it felt like a moment of healing, forgiveness. He smiled from under the mask—full-face oxygen now—and said, "Maybe tomorrow will be a better day."

He tried his best to breathe with the oxygen mask, even though the respiratory therapist said that the velocity was like hanging your head out the window of a speeding car. He was afraid he would fall asleep and not be able to breathe. Finally, after nearly 48 hours, he texted around 3 a.m. to say, "I think I need to go onto the ventilator." I replied, "OK. Tell the nurse," and he responded, "Will you?"

So I called the unit, getting up and dressing. We got to the hospital within the half hour. I was glad Tom was with me, that he had the car, and that I didn't have to be alone. Vic and Janet were already there, and we were all with him before the procedure. We stayed in the waiting room until they called us back about an hour-and-a-half later. John was resting peacefully.

Vic and Janet left later that morning; I stayed through the end of the week. Tom had left, too. I was glad to be by myself and on my own. John needed my focus. I was so afraid that he was not going to make it through this. He was so very sick.

Allison—June 17, Year One

Back at work, my cell phone buzzed on my desk; these days it was never far from my hand. This time it was from a minister-friend, calling to ask how John was doing, and how was I. I had just gotten several texts from Vic who was taking his week at Duke hospital. I had felt the despondency coming through his texted phrases.

"He's bad," I half-gasped into the phone. "I don't know how he is hanging on. I don't know how he can keep doing this. I don't know how *we* can keep doing this."

My friend made sounds of acknowledgement. No one knew what to say anymore. John had now been hospitalized two months. Two days before, doctors removed the ventilator tube from his throat (for the second time during this stay at Duke), but now, again, his breathing was worse. The numbers kept falling.

"I don't know what to do," I whispered into the phone. I often felt like I didn't have enough breath either. Not enough to talk or cry; just enough for shallow gasps to keep making my body move through the days, through the functions of holding down a job, of holding myself together.

"I am praying to be willing to let him go. What do I need to do? How can it keep on like this?"

Though he had no magic words, I could feel my friend's empathy coming through the phone. Finally saying he would call my ex-husband, he hung up, and I went back to the motions of my job. A key fob lying on my desk caught my eye. Earlier that day, a hospital employee I didn't know well had brought it to me. Done in cloisonné, it had pictures of Our Lady on each side. I put it on my key ring, grateful for the prayers of the person who had given it to me.

It was a Thursday of this my week to work, his father's to stand vigil at Duke. I had left Duke on Sunday, after John was put on the ventilator early the previous Thursday. They tried to take him off it on Tuesday afternoon, but he had to go back on in less than 36 hours. That was the only awake time I missed, those 36 hours. They said he was very brave, only asking for Vic to pray.

I was to go back to Durham on Saturday. Anne was leaving tomorrow for a trip to Europe with her parents. I knew she shouldn't go, that she probably wouldn't see John alive again.

The next day, Friday, I talked to Vic and again heard the quiet despair in his voice. Anne was already at the airport in D.C. I called my friend Libba and asked her to drive me up to Duke that afternoon. We each left work and got on the road by four for the four-hour drive. We made it for part of the last visiting time in ICU that night.

Back by John's bedside, where I'd come to stand many times, I reached across tubes to touch his hair. It was long before his sickness, and now with two months' growth, it was to his shoulders. Frequently, the ICU nurses washed it, attaching a plastic basin at the head of the bed. Often nurse Zeliah French-braided it. John, who hated to be fussed over, would not believe the tender care he received to every part of his body. Nurses constantly rotated and turned his six-foot frame; he never had a single skin breakdown.

Vic left on Saturday, to get back to his other responsibilities. My friend Libba left, too, and I was alone with my boy. And the nurses. ICU visitation was strict, and I was there from 10:30 a.m. to 2 p.m., 4:30 to 6:30 p.m., 7:30 to 9 p.m. Each time I went back, it was with trepidation; *What would I find? What would be different?* And each time John's nurse was there to tell me the latest details of his condition. I knew they cared about him, and that they cared about me. They were some of the kindest, most competent people I have ever known.

Dutifully every day, I wrote on "the charts." When John first got to Duke, artist Megan, along with Anne, created poster board charts, dating back to his initial hospitalization. In different colors of markers, we logged each day, by date, the amount of prednisone, Cytoxan and blood thinner, the number of blood transfusions and plasmapheresis treatments, the names of multiple antibiotics, and the various procedures he was receiving. Everyone marveled at the charts that were taped on the walls and glass doors of his room. We kept them with a certain reverence, no matter which of us was "on duty." I guess it was our attempt to get our arms around something too huge to handle.

The doctors liked the charts, too. It was a help to the many specialists to see at a glance what had transpired since April 13. Unbelievable, really. Teams of them—internists for the ICU, nephrologists, infectious disease specialists, hematologists, and our favorites, the rheumatologists—treated John. Respiratory therapists were in and out frequently, as were pharmacists, who were an integral part of the medical team and closely monitored the interaction and effects of each medication on various parts of John's system. We all wore yellow paper gowns and yellow latex gloves and later, yellow masks. Besides being so immuno-compromised, John had several highly commutable infectious diseases, which often attacked long-term hospital patients.

One doctor regularly commented to me, "He has such a wonderful family!" Maybe that was something she didn't have or perhaps didn't see too often with patients, but it deeply gratified me. Ever since the divorce when John's world changed dramatically at age 14, our family had been fragmented. That we could all come together with such strength around him had to be healing. I prayed so.

I believe it also helped with his care. With one of us always there, looking at the medical team with eyes that plead, *Please don't stop. Do something,* it was harder for them to quit trying. And they never did. He had the best medical care in the world.

Through these June days, I stood by John's bed and told him everything I could think of—how well USC was doing in baseball, what was happening in the World Cup. He had played soccer since he was four, and it was his favorite sport. His soccer foot got him the position of place kicker for the varsity football team when he was in tenth grade. I told him of all the people who were praying for him, and I read to him the many entries on CarePages each day. Mostly I prayed. *Please God, don't let John die.* I wore a rosewood rosary that Tom had given me, and I, Baptist-raised, spent a lot of time talking to Mother Mary who suffered the loss of a Son. At the bedside or hundreds of miles away, we prayed and kept the vigil.

Allison—June 22, Year One

I pushed through the revolving front door of Duke University Medical Center where John lay motionless with a ventilator breathing for him, tubes going in and out various parts of his body, and machines throbbing around him. I had stood by him, gowned and gloved, stroking his forehead or his long curls, talking softly, for the first segment of the day's visiting hours. It was now after 2 p.m. and the sun and heat beat against me as I exited the building. I squinted at my cell phone, beginning to text as I walked. Over one shoulder was a bag of the day's necessities—laptop, water bottle, money, journal, hotel key. I had on backless, wooden sandals that clacked as I pounded down the sidewalk.

I texted simultaneously my daughter Megan, ex-husband Vic, two cousins, a close friend, and two co-workers, giving them the latest report. It was always worse—even when we all wondered how it could get much worse.

I walked more than a mile to a nearby shopping center to buy lunch. The heat was suffocating. I shifted my bag to the other shoulder as I waited at a crosswalk. Doctors in white coats and students walked along the sidewalks, also hunched against the force of the heat. I welcomed it. Anything, to beat against the cold terror that raged around me. *He's dying, he's dying, he's dying,* screamed inside my head.

I strode back to the hospital, other side of the street, now carrying my take-out lunch as well. I bought a drink at the lobby gift shop, ate in the lobby, responded to work messages on my laptop, until 4:30 p.m. and I could go back into ICU. The routine was essential, a guardrail against uncontrolled panic.

John was even worse than when I left him. The spinal tap showed cryptococcus in his spinal fluid, as well as what's been raging in his lungs. They started him on CVVHD, a type of continuous dialysis gentler on the body than regular dialysis. He was on a new drug—an antifungal—plus an antiviral, and getting two more units of blood. They were still adjusting his sedation.

The clinical people were always so calm. They spoke in numbers and polysyllabic words and I clung to each phrase, trying to deduce a relative meaning.

Lauren, my favorite nurse, was on today. Wearing her usual pearl earrings, her dark hair pulled back, she was beautiful, poised, and professional. She was one-on-one today with John and her eyes rarely left him as she checked all the devices surrounding him. Now it was difficult to stand beside him, there was so much equipment, but I tried to squeeze in. Lauren was concerned that she was going to need more access for additional meds, so soon someone came in to place another PICC line in his arm. Then another Alaris pump was hung. There were six of them now, double-decked onto three poles, for all his meds to drip in.

The charge nurse burst in. She had become a friend. Her words penetrated my understanding where the clinical terms could not. She asked me how long it would take the rest of the family to get here and told me she was going to call John's girlfriend who'd left three days earlier on a trip to Europe, to let her know there had been another change.

"Don't call them yet," she said as she left. "I will let you know."

Suddenly Lauren was calling, sternly, "John! John!" and calmly told me he was losing blood pressure. I switched my eyes to fix on that monitor and watched the numbers fall. Now she was at the end of the bed, lowering it until the head almost touched the floor, still calling his name. Another nurse rushed in, and Lauren sent her for a medication to elevate his blood pressure; soon that too was going in his vein. The numbers read 60/40. Then slowly they began creeping back up. The other nurse asked what could she do, but Lauren was in control. I had been pressed back against the wall. I realized that I needed to breathe. Neither was I conscious I was praying; it was unconscious and constant.

Soon after that, it was 6:30 p.m. and time for me to leave the ICU again. I removed the yellow paper gown and latex gloves that everyone had to wear to enter the room and threw them into the overflowing trash container. "I'll be back at 7:30," I said, hating that Lauren would be gone then.

I walked out the back of the hospital this time, my evening route, across the Duke campus to the chapel. It was at least three miles there and back, and it took up the hour until the evening visiting time. Part of the route was through a construction breezeway. It was dusty and still hot as I marched along my path. I remembered the last thing John had said before going on the ventilator this time: "I don't want to die." I texted Megan and Vic and my cousins, Elaine and Diane, and told them this latest, my fingers typing as fast as my pace. Everyone was praying. Megan said, "I am glad he has his strong Momma there with him, keeping him alive."

I didn't feel strong. I didn't feel much of anything, detached from myself. I only felt John, as though I was acutely tied to his energy.

Approaching the chapel, I looked up at the enormous stone cathedral that sat in the center of the campus, its spire visible from many angles. I pulled open the heavy wooden doors and entered the cool twilight of the interior. Stained glass windows lined the walls. I walked down the flagstone aisle, even my noisy shoes muffled by the vastness of the vaulted interior. I went all the way to the front, up the stone steps and knelt on the cold marble. Here I prayed, consciously, verbally. *Please God, let him live. Please don't take our boy.* These days I prayed a lot to Mother Mary, too, figuring she understood what it was like to love—and lose—a son. I asked her to intervene for the life of my son.

After a time, I got up, going out a side door. One of John's doctors has told me about another chapel, a smaller one in the Divinity School building. I entered next door, looking for it, followed the sound of voices, and came to the top of stairs. I could see into the chapel; there was a class in there and a man was at the podium talking about death. Caught by the topic, I sat on the top step and listened through the open door. He spoke about how Jesus is with us, at the cross, the tomb, and the resurrection. I waited, straining to hear a message. Was God telling me, *Yes, John is going to die?* But I didn't hear anything.

I got up and walked on, and almost immediately, my cell phone rang. It was an old friend of my ex-husband, whom I hadn't heard from in the decade since our divorce. He was calling to tell me how much he was praying for John. Somehow, the synchronicity of his call was the message I was listening for. God was actively present with me, and hearing all our prayers.

Back in ICU, John was quiet and there was no change. I stayed the allowed hour and left, calling the hotel shuttle from the lobby. In the womb of my room at the Millennium Hotel where Internet service was almost nil and cell phone calls impossible, I closed my eyes. But sleep eluded as my mind tried to fathom the events of the past ten weeks.

John—June, Year One

A few weeks later I came very close to dying myself. The gold standard of Wegener's treatment, Cytoxan, had not been working for me. After oral and IV treatments in Greenville and at Duke over several months I wasn't getting better. My lungs were still bleeding and I was drowning in the blood. By this time I was wearing a mask that was comparable to sticking your head out of a car window while moving at 80mph. With this mask on, I couldn't eat or drink because the force of the oxygen could push any food or water into my lungs. It was also impossible for me to talk, so I began writing short notes to my family when I needed to say something. Talk about frustrating! In the time it took to write what I was thinking, everyone in the room would've tried a dozen times to guess what it was. I couldn't sleep because I had to keep trying to breathe.

The night I was induced into a medical coma was a long one. My body was almost completely exhausted from lack of sleep and nourishment, I had several bags of meds dripping into multiple IVs, and I was scared. I knew I couldn't keep it up much longer so I texted my family, who were staying in town, and told them I needed them to come back as soon as possible regardless that visiting hours were over and wouldn't start again until morning. When everyone was there, I told them how bad it was and asked my dad if I should just go on the ventilator to be able to go sleep. He said yes, that my body was tired and sleeping would give it energy to fight. I remember asking if he thought I would wake up if I went to sleep. I was aware that "going to sleep" was a lot more serious than it sounded. I didn't know what would happen when I quit fighting. He told me I would wake up and it would feel like I had just been asleep for a few hours, like it always did when they put me under. Looking back I wish I hadn't asked that question. What if I hadn't woken up? Would he think about that for the rest of his life?

As soon as I made that decision, my room was filled with doctors and nurses ready to pounce on my near lifeless body. I was intubated and then a couple of weeks later, I was trached and then "PEGed." 'Course I was unconscious.

Anne was in Europe with her family, a trip planned in advance and something I wholeheartedly wanted her to do, seeing as she had basically stopped her own life to be by my side constantly throughout the whole experience. Knowing she wouldn't get it, I sent a text that night saying I loved her.

Allison—June, Year One

I climbed out of a dream: *Earthquake. The earth shakes and splits open before me and all is falling, slanting sideways, nothing is stable. I try to find a foothold, and then the tidal wave is rushing in . . . .* In the semi-darkness of the room, thick curtains holding back the daylight, I reached for my phone. There were no messages, but texts don't always come through in these rooms. Actual calls never did. I would go get coffee in the lobby, check my phone and email first. There was time before the morning visit period.

Time. Time itself changed on April 13, 2010. Before that, it was just normal time filled with work and goals and thoughts like, *Can I adjust to this new job? Will I ever marry again? I wish Megan lived in Greenville. I wish I had a workable retirement plan.* Then it was April 13, and time became Before John Got Sick and Since John Got Sick. Life became meted out by that demarcation line. Normal and Not.

I didn't wonder the theological "why" of all this, but more just the specifics of why Wegener's—a disease so rare as to be almost unknown. Doctors had plumbed us all for possible causes, and we came up with nothing. Their determination was "idiopathic," meaning "no known cause." Or, as a doctor said, "It makes us all look like idiots." After steeling myself many nights during his teenage years for the feared call of a tragic accident, and then to have him happy and healthy at 26 and be struck by a random killer—it seemed incomprehensible.

Soon I caught the Millennium Hotel's shuttle for Duke hospital. There, John continued to fight, with fever and infection "hiding in every nook and cranny of his body," as one doctor phrased it. Another doctor, standing beside me at John's bed said, "I'm sorry it had to come to this." I hated it that he was so battered and bloodied; his weight had dropped to 140 pounds. He looked like he'd been in battle. Then I realized he had—the battle for his life.

He was getting a central line in now, and then they would do a tracheostomy. He had been on the ventilator too long for it to be safe, so they would make a small slit in his throat for the trach to enter. I had the worst time with this than anything else he had been through. I had worked in hospitals too long, seen too many people on trachs having to be permanently cared for or maybe progressing to talk through an artificial "voice box" outside of their throats. I understood why it is necessary, but I was distraught. As I waited in the upper lobby, my phone rang. It was Kelli, the young resident from Greenville with whom we had serendipitous encounters the past few months. I told her what was happening and she told me, "Allison, it will be *fine*. I just saw a 19-year-old in OB clinic. She had a tracheotomy a year ago, and now the only way you can tell is by the small scar on her throat." Another gift from God, this call, from someone who had not called me before or since.

Our pastor-friend came twice to Duke to visit. My friend Ellen drove up. She, too, stroked John's hair and told him of activities of his friends in Greenville; she had known him since he was three years old. I told her that the team was worried that all the strong antibiotics were killing his already weakened kidneys. She exclaimed, "Oh Allison! We will get him a kidney," which oddly comforted me.

The waiting was interminable. Every day. Yet the team never gave up. Neither did John.

More blood transfusions, this time also platelets and plasma. Another bronchoscopy and a lumbar puncture to check for MRSA, methicillin-resistant staphyloccoccus aureus. They mentioned putting in a PEG (percutaneius endoscopic gastrostomy) tube in his stomach for feeding, since he hadn't had much nutrition for weeks. I could hardly bear the thought of this either, which screamed long-term nursing home care to me.

It was likely the Wegener's again that was killing him. The ICU doctors had turned back to Dr. Allen, the rheumatologist, after ruling out or containing other possibilities.

"It's all on you," I heard the head ICU doctor tell her and saw his slight, sardonic smile. Her shoulders lifted and fell with her sigh. She was considering Rituxan, or rituximab, a drug just coming out of clinical trials for Wegener's, since the Cytoxan didn't seem to be working. Such a miracle that she was here, that June was the month for her hospital rotation, and that she cared so much about us all. She had given me both her cell phone number and her home phone number to call anytime.

I just wanted him to wake up and be okay. I prayed for the medical team to make the right judgments and take the best action for him.

Allison—June 27, Year One

It was a Sunday, my ninth day this stint of waking up at the Millennium and catching the shuttle to Duke University Medical Center. Vic and Janet came up yesterday to take their turn, but I couldn't leave. If force of spirit had any power over death, then I had resolutely stood by John the past days to fend it off. I couldn't leave yet.

The Bufords surprised me by driving up to Duke today. Dee and Tom, who had loved John for years and helped him through college, stayed at his bedside until the 2 p.m. visitation was over. I went with them to lunch and then they dropped me off at the hotel on their way back to Greenville; I would go back to the hospital for the 4:30 visiting time. As I was entering my room, the hotel phone was ringing. It was a doctor calling me from the ICU, telling me to come back to the hospital right away.

I rushed to the front desk. Shuttles ran only every half hour.

"I have to get back to the hospital immediately!" I said. The clerk rounded up a driver and soon I was running through the hospital lobby. I pressed the wall plate at ICU, not waiting to use the intercom. I rounded the corner to John's cubicle, and Vic came forward to meet me, slowly shaking his head.

"NOOOO!" The scream that erupted from my usually quiet self could be heard throughout the ICU. Vic immediately said, "No, no, not THAT. He's just very bad."

Then the doctor who called me, a woman pulmonologist whom I didn't remember seeing before, was in front of me, talking to me, explaining that John was barely breathing even with the ventilator, that they were all working with him. She led me to a chair across from John's room. Janet sat in the chair beside me, and then Vic. She took my hand.

We could see into John's area, and it was like a scene from "ER," with at least a dozen people, gowned, masked, and gloved, rushing in and out, calling for various equipment and medication. All I could pray was to John, "Please don't go."

The charge nurse appeared and said, "You should call your daughter." She was at Sewanee this summer, and it would take nine hours for her and her husband Haynes to arrive.

We sat. Periodically there was a break in the crowd around John, and I could see blood coming up and out into the ventilator tube. He couldn't get enough oxygen for the bleeding. I felt the presence of the Angel of Death in the room.

Then the doctor came out to explain that they were going to try to get him onto an oscillator, a ventilator used for pediatric patients. Because his lungs were so damaged from the Wegener's and the cryptococcal infection, the regular ventilator was beating them up. The oscillator would blow tiny puffs of air, three hundred per minute, into his lungs. However, since this was an unnatural process that his body would fight, he would have to be given a paralytic. She warned us of the risks, including paralysis he might not recover from. We said, "Do anything you can. Please."

Sometime later, the doctor came to tell us she was leaving to attend to another patient, and that they hadn't yet been able to successfully get John onto the oscillator. The final alternative to control the bleeding was something called Factor 7. Again we said please do it, not really sure what that means, other than a chance.

"I need to call Anne," I said. She was in some part of Europe with her family, not scheduled to be back for several more days, but I had a number to reach her father. When he answered, I told him briefly what was happening. Then in the background, I heard Anne's screams, an echo of my own from two hours earlier.

I stepped into the hall to call my friend Libba, who said she and her husband Bob would leave Greenville immediately for Duke. Then I called my childhood friend Sally, to tell her I wasn't coming home and to please keep feeding my cat. She asked how he was, and I said, "He's dying," before my voice broke into tears. I suddenly had an image of pulling into my driveway days later and John no longer being on this earth . . . . It was an unbearable thought. "I don't know what I will do," I said, and I heard her whimpering, two little girls crying together.

Two more hours passed as the team worked on John. Apparently it wasn't easy to get clearance to administer Factor VII. One dose cost $7,000. If ordered and then not used, it had to be wasted. We waited. Then a doctor came to tell us that a respiratory therapist had gotten John onto the oscillator, that he was "somewhat stable, but could teeter either way." Looking into the room, I sensed that the presence of Death had receded.

I saw that only the nurse was with John, so I went to the door and asked if I could be with him. She said, "Of course," so I gowned up and went in. I tried my best to tell him good-bye but I couldn't. I left, and Vic took my place.

That evening, the staff opened a conference room for us. A few friends arrived. I was curled up on the floor when Megan and Haynes got there around 1:30 a.m. After they went in to see John for a while, we went to the hotel to rest for a few hours.

Again, John held off death. There was very little change as we all waited.

I called my friend Elizabeth, and Tom. They had been praying non-stop. Elizabeth told me that she believed that John was going to be fine, that he would come through this. It was hard to even hear that. I wanted to argue with her. She hadn't seen what I had. She couldn't know how bad he was.

On Monday, Dr. Allen and the rheumatology fellow taking care of John came into the conference room to talk to us. The fellow, a lovely Indian woman who had prayed with John, could not look at any of us. Dr. Allen, with calm concern, laid out the particulars of John's current condition and projections for the long term. We listened and asked questions and I took notes:

Possible kidney failure—dialysis, transplant

Lungs—some damage/scarring from the infections,
      Wegener's, ventilator

Brain?—periods of low blood pressure and low oxygen

Heart—good

Gastro—don't know. Ulcers?

Vocal chords—damage (and stenosis from the trach?)

Muscular—rehab, nutrition

Blood clots—filter in place; continue on Coumadin

Chronic pain—tolerance? Addiction?

Later I wrote: *John is still here. They don't want us to talk to him or try to rouse him at all today. The paralytic is keeping him on the oscillating respirator. All I pray is that he lives; it will be a joy to deal with anything else necessary.*

We waited . . . Monday, Tuesday. On Wednesday morning, Anne and her mother arrived. We met them in the cafeteria before the 10:30 visiting time. Anne was silent and couldn't eat as we waited. Haynes picked up a small container of trail mix and the cashier told him, "Seven dollars." He said, "I'm not paying *that*!" and put it back on the rack. We all returned to the conference room they were still letting us use.

As we sat idly, Anne's mother handed her a cup of trail mix, encouraging her to eat something. She passed it around to the rest of us. Haynes took a handful and said, "I feel like I should pay you a dollar," and we all laughed. The comic relief was so appreciated.

Suddenly, it was a repeat of Sunday. The nurse came in to tell us that John was barely breathing. They were going to do another bronchoscopy. Again there were chairs placed for us in the ICU hallway. This time as I sat between Megan and Anne, the thought hit me that, unlike Sunday, everyone was here. *He waited until everyone got here* . . . . I could not endure it any more.

An ICU doctor stepped over to check on me and asked "What do you need?"

I said, "I need to YELL." She nodded.

I left and went to the small hospital chapel a couple of floors above. It was empty.

The wood-paneled room was round and non-denominational, with prayer rugs and red cushioned benches lining the walls. I leaned against the wall and tried to pray. My pain was that I could not let him go; my angst, that he'd always said about me, "She tells me what I need to know," and I couldn't this time. *I am afraid I am letting him down, because I can't accept this, can't let him go,* I wailed inside. *Am I supposed to "let him go?" How can I possibly do that? I can't, and I can no longer watch him die; it is too impossibly hard.*

Then I was crying, face down on the cushioned bench. My cries wrenched from my pent-up terror, releasing the despair. I heard a small sound behind the wall and then felt the presence of someone beside me, but my sobs didn't abate. Then a soft voice spoke, "You don't have to say anything and I'll leave if you want, but I want you to know that you are not alone."

I was too distraught even to care. The stranger touched my hair. At some point, I thought that whoever this person was, she didn't know me and I would never see her again, so it wouldn't matter if I said whatever I wanted.

So I sat up and blurted out, "My son is dying. It almost happened Sunday, and now it's happening *again*. They are doing all they can, and he *is dying!* And he and my daughter are all I've ever had! Parents gone and no siblings . . . and now *John* is dying!"

She only listened, but I could feel her agonizing with me. Finally I was calmer and could sit up and take the tissues she offered me. I had the sense that I could not bear *this* any longer—this seeming false-death process, and

39

that I didn't have to. John would not want this pain for me. I decided that I was leaving the next day, my birthday. I asked her if she would walk me back to ICU, because I wasn't sure if I'd be able to. As we walked, she told me she was a lay minister come to offer communion to church members. I never even asked her name, this angel hidden in the closet behind my grief.

Back at ICU, I learned that they got out a mucus plug and old blood during the bronchoscopy, and John held on. I called my co-workers and asked them to come get me the next day. Before I left, I handed Vic a note and said, "I am leaving tomorrow; I can't watch anymore." I was spent.

He glanced at the note, and I reiterated what was on it. "They will ask about an autopsy; we don't need one. That's the name of the mortuary. Please call Baxter about doing the funeral at First Baptist." He nodded, folded the note, and put it in his pocket.

The next day, my fifty-seventh birthday, co-workers Sue and Andrea came to Duke to get me. Andrea went back to ICU with me as I told her, "I need someone to validate this for me."

John's cubicle looked like something from Star Wars. There was so much equipment it was difficult to get into the room. We put on the yellow gowns, gloves, and masks and got as close as we could. Three sets of triple-tiered Alaris pumps dripped various medications into numerous IV's. Tubes were coming out of every orifice. The machines hummed and hissed, and lights blinked red, green, and yellow all around him.

I reached to stroke his forehead and told him I was leaving and would see him later.

Several of us went to lunch at Nosh, in a half-hearted acknowledgement of my birthday, and then I left with Sue and Andrea to return to Greenville. Later they told me that they thought I would get a call on the four-hour drive home that John had passed.

Allison—July, Year One

I left for Durham today, my friend Catherine driving me up, after being away for ten days. Numb and exhausted, I had gone through the motions of work. Work was always intense, with many details of managing multiple projects, plus the hour travel time each day. I still felt new at this job, that I had to prove myself, and that this was not yet my community.

John had held on. Janet sent me a text yesterday saying he would need to come back to Greenville for rehabilitation or long-term care, that he would not be able to go to Franklin as had been offered weeks ago.

He was off the oscillator and back on the regular ventilator. The infections were better and the ICU pharmacist was working to decrease his sedation. He didn't have the horrible withdrawal he had last time in Greenville. A special psychiatrist had been in to also help manage medications to begin to address the post-traumatic stress syndrome. They told us we would have to address our PTSD, too. Pharmacy was such an integral part of the team there. Their contribution to the doctors regarding particular drugs and their interactions was not something we'd seen before.

The previous day the doctors had started John on rituximab, the new treatment. It was just coming out of clinical trials for treating Wegener's. He got the treatments by infusion. The nasal tube had been removed and he now had a PEG for tube feedings.

Two of John's friends came to visit. I waited in the hall as the nurse helped them gown up and took them into his cubicle. Suddenly one of them was hurrying back out, wide-eyed, still wearing his isolation garb. The nurse quietly caught up with him, helping him out of the paper gown, handing him Kleenex. I heard her so calmly validating the shock and terror he must be feeling. After a bit, he decided to re-gown and go back in. There was nothing about John's situation that was not ghastly.

Allison—July, Year One

John was frustrated today at not being able to communicate. But how amazing it was to see him sitting up in bed and showing appropriate emotion! Anne was present most of the time, too, so that helped. It would be easier for me to leave this time.

I realized again the metaphor of earthquake. Megan and I had both had dreams about it. When everything solid beneath you moves, keeps shuddering, and finally starts to settle in a totally new fashion. That was what these months felt like.

John—Coma, June/July, Year One

Many people have asked me what it was like to be in a coma—what I could see, hear, feel while I was this close to death. Some are just curious, some are worried for their future, and some have been beside a loved one is this situation and want to know if they were heard. For better or worse, I don't remember anything. It's probably a blessing. My body was basically being tortured and my mind needed rest, but I've always wished there had been *something*. It would've been nice to have seen Pop-Pop, or Jeremy, or at least a glimpse of the creeks at Litchfield where I fell in love with the coast while vacationing with Smith and his family. Anything that would've let me know it will be okay when my time really comes.

On the day he visited, my uncle who's always "seen" angels, saw two angels working on me while I was under. He said the room was crowded with doctors, nurses, and machines, but the two, reddish-orange angels kept their heads down and focused on my body toward my head.

While I didn't fly on a unicorn or smoke a blunt with B.I.G. and Pac in heaven, I can say it was much better than the first time I woke up from being intubated several months earlier. I basically woke up a little bewildered but in a good mood. There were a few tubes and holes that I didn't remember, so I knew something serious had happened. Somehow Anne and my family kept their composure and did an amazing job just letting me slowly come back to my senses on my own without jumping on me or yelling at me for almost leaving them. There was definitely a fog. But things were brighter and calmer than the first time.

The first time I was intubated was dark and confusing. Instead of my mind being blank, it was working overtime creating several dreams or illusions that I thought were absolutely real. It was the closest my mind could comprehend to what Hell would be. No friends, no family, no food, no water, and an invariable sense of eternal torture and death. Although much shorter, the first experience in Greenville felt like multiple lifetimes, whereas the Duke coma could've been a day in my mind.

Before I was induced into the coma at Duke, I had been looking forward to my Gamecocks playing in the College World Series (which they won) and World Cup soccer. Watching TV is basically the only thing you can do in the hospital, and daytime TV gets pretty monotonous, so something new was a big deal. It may even have allowed me to keep track of days for the first time in months—but it wasn't to be. Before either series started I called my family and was put on the ventilator.

Giving up never crossed my mind. It took a while before I even realized how serious things had been, and it still didn't register that I was in any kind of mortal danger. It took my breath away the first time I heard how long I was actually unconscious. The idea that I was closer to dead than living remains one of the hardest things to face and because of that, I've almost completely blocked out what I was told.

Besides my family members and Anne speaking to and praying over my motionless body on a daily basis, several friends came to see me. Right before I woke up, two of my oldest and best friends came up in response to a CarePages update my mom sent out. She was rightfully afraid that I wouldn't live more than a day or two, so they came to say goodbye. The Duke doctors had told my family there was nothing else they could do. I was being battered by the machines that were keeping me alive, and I still couldn't breathe on my own.

Whether luck or divine miracle, a respiratory therapist working there was just as stubborn as I was about not giving up. His last-ditch effort was to get me on a machine called an oscillator that the attending doctor had thought of. From what I've heard since then, an oscillator is like a ventilator, but instead of your lungs opening and closing, it blasts air in at several hundred breaths per minute. This basically kept my lungs open and let them get some rest from opening and closing. Like so many other times, without that one idea and one machine and one person, I wouldn't be alive.

Shortly after being switched from the ventilator to the oscillator, my lungs got enough rest to start working on their own. It would be a never-ending battle with thousands of pitfalls ahead, but I wasn't done living yet. There were still too many things I wanted to do, places to see, people to meet. And I didn't want to die without at least seeing the beach again.

I wasn't ready to die.

I wasn't the person I wanted to be.

I hadn't done anything yet.

I hadn't been anywhere.

I still didn't have a dog.

There were too many people I had to see again, and I had too many questions.

There were too many things I hadn't told people, and no one single person had ever known everything about me.

Nobody had told me what I was supposed to do next.

Was I ever going to see anybody again?

What was the point?

If that had been the end, would it/I have felt different?

Allison—July 31, Year One

Off the ventilator, off dialysis, and back to a regular room! John called me today to actually talk—not just text. Anne took a picture of him on a tall walker. He had made it five laps around the hallways with a physical therapist.

They were making plans to discharge him to a lesser level of care. The social worker wanted him to stay in Durham, but he was so ready to be in Greenville where friends were. We were trying to get him in the rehab hospital here. I was returning to Duke the following day.

The next day, John's doctor on the unit came in—her name was Dr. Jolly—and told him he could expect full remission from the Wegener's and likely complete recovery. It was too much for me to absorb. This seemed normal to John who had waked from a Rip Van Winkle sleep, without awareness of the passage of time, and was ready to jump back into his life. The rehab hospital could take him in about a week, as soon as he transitioned off the IV and onto oral blood thinner, and his INR number was within acceptable ranges. As Megan said, by phone, "It's just a plain old miracle!"

I was leaving after the weekend and Megan would join Anne for the last few days of John's stay here, ending this part of the journey as they began it with him.

Allison—August 6, Year One

John arrived at Roger C. Peace Rehab hospital in Greenville late on a Friday afternoon, in the front seat of Anne's car! Finally having gotten the discharge that day and not willing to wait on ambulance arrangements, they took off, Megan following in her car. I tried to block out my worry and fatigue and just focused on the miracle.

He worked so hard in several hours daily of intensive therapy that he was able to be released in a week. He left with only a cane. Since arrangements for his going to North Carolina had not worked out, he would come home to me. Anne was already staying with me, in my small two-bedroom, one-bath house. I was glad he was coming but I felt inadequate, even ashamed, that my accommodations were so meager. I worried that I wouldn't have enough means to support him.

That night, he insisted on going to his favorite restaurant, The Peddler. All of the "team" went, plus Megan's husband Haynes, Vic and Janet, and our friends the Gowers. John walked with his cane and managed to navigate part of a steak. And the next day, my cousins Diane and Elaine and her daughter Meredith came and took us to the Green Room for lunch. I felt worried and confused. As we were leaving, I asked my cousins, "I need a reality check here. Just a short time ago, he really was dying—right?"

"Yes!" was their immediate response. Diane told me that while she had been on her trip to Yosemite and sometimes out of phone contact, Elaine had arranged with Diane's son in Florida to gather and send her clothes for a funeral so that she could fly straight to Atlanta and then come here. Everyone agreed it was a miracle; people have referred to him as Lazarus. Yet they understood my gnawing fear that all might not be well yet.

John—Rehab, August, Year One

Toward the end of my hospitalization at Duke, my sense of smell was super human! It was after I woke up from the coma, so it could've had something to do with sensory deprivation, but it made already terrible food completely inedible. When I could remember, I would ask for the lid of the cafeteria tray to be lifted outside of my room so it wouldn't overwhelm my olfactory sense. I still had a feeding tube in my stomach at this point, and I could swear I constantly smelled the formula oozing out of the bag directly into my stomach. It reminded me of something by Edgar Allen Poe I read growing up; my own senses at odds with my brain with no one else able to verify the agony of The Tell Tale Smell. It kept the Catch 22 of not-getting-the-disgusting-feeding-tube-removed-until-I-could-gain-weight versus not-gaining-weight-until-I-got-the-disgusting-feeding-tube-removed in play for longer than expected. Chewing and swallowing became such a problem that all I could get down were protein shakes. And I hated them. After a while a doctor told me if I could get two of the protein drinks down in one day, he would remove the tube. I did, and to my surprise, he pulled about two inches of tubing out my stomach with a single gloved hand and that was that. If I had known it was that simple, I probably would've done it myself much sooner.

Each ounce of those drinks counted. At that point I weighed around 145 pounds. My muscles had so atrophied during the coma and from the paralytics that I could barely sit up in bed, and it would take weeks to walk again.

My average weight before I was hospitalized was around 185 pounds. Because I hadn't been eating due to pain and fatigue, I believe I was initially admitted at about 175. After the first few weeks and several days in a row on 1,000 milligrams of steroids, I began having unexplained pains on my sides. In hindsight, I now know that this pain was actually my skin stretching to make room for the 235-pound body that would eventually lie in my hospital bed. Between the swollen ankles, stretch marks, nausea and extreme sense of smell, I'm closer to knowing what pregnancy feels like than any man should be. Let me say for the record, be nice to your pregnant wives, guys.

Once the feeding tube was removed and my appetite slowly returned, we began getting better and better news from the doctors. All I wanted to do was "go home," which meant, of course, back to a hospital in Greenville. So my doctors, my family, and I began doing what each of us could to get me there. A few weeks later the trach was removed from my neck, we were told my Wegener's was in remission, and I was allowed to get in my girlfriend's car and ride back to Roger C. Peace, a rehabilitation hospital in Greenville.

When I left Duke for Roger C. Peace, I had a hole in my throat from the tracheostomy; a hole in my stomach from the feeding tube; my thumb, index and middle finger of both hands had nerve damage from drawing arterial blood and had lost at least 75 percent sensation; the tops of my feet had nerve damage and were extremely sensitive; I had a central line dangling from my chest; I was at least forty pounds underweight; and because I was immunosuppressed, I had been infected with cryptococcal meningitis and other resistant infections.

But the Wegener's was in remission and I felt hopeful. At Roger C. Peace, amazing staff taught me how to walk, talk, bathe, eat, and generally function as a human being again.

At times I was miserable. I had lost all control in my life. If I needed to do any of the things above, I had to have help. As an independent and fairly private guy who ran track, wrestled, played soccer and football in high school and grew up playing Little League baseball, church league basketball, and soccer year around for a multiple-time state-championship-winning team, it was a serious adjustment. They didn't even want me to stand up by myself, much less walk. And I had to press on the bandage covering the hole in my throat to talk, similar to long-time smokers with no voice box.

There had been indecision about where and whom I would live with. Somewhere along the way it was determined I would stay at my mom's house. All my belongings had been in a storage unit since the time it became obvious I wouldn't be leaving the hospital anytime soon. I couldn't have lived on my own anyway.

I was petrified that it would start all over again, that I'd forget to take a medicine or something and be thrown back into the cycle. Which happened in a way.

3

Complications

Allison—August 20, Year One

JOHN HAD BEEN HOME a week. On Friday he left unexpectedly; his dad came to take him to North Carolina for the weekend. Suddenly it was like he was five and I was afraid for him to go. He was still so pale and weak. The other night he was grouchy, insisting that I go out late and look for over-the-counter medication for stomach pain. I had been hesitant—he was already on about 30 meds—but I did, nevertheless. Anne had gone home to her parents for the weekend.

I had been able to get John's disability application processed while he was at Duke; it was approved in a month's time, something apparently unheard of. They must have thought he was dying and it wouldn't matter anyway. A Blue Cross-Blue Shield case manager had called me soon after John arrived at Duke. Then I had just been glad to know that his work insurance was continuing to pay. Later I learned that case managers were assigned to individuals only after a bill passed the million-dollar amount. The Greenville hospital had helped to arrange Medicaid after John had been hospitalized a month, to cover hospital balances. All his mail had been going to his apartment, and we had never gotten it. I'm grateful we never even knew all the costs.

On Sunday I met Vic and Janet halfway to pick up John in Asheville. He had been very sick Saturday—nausea and throwing up. I waited at the designated spot for two hours. Vic called to say that John had been too sick and weak to travel.

Finally they pulled into the parking lot and I opened the car door. John was leaned back in the passenger seat, a basin in his lap. He was pale and shaking and too weak to move.

"We have to take him straight to the hospital!" I said and refused to do anything but go back to my car. "I will follow you."

48

After several hours in the Asheville emergency room, with some tests and blood work, they had given him something for pain and nausea and wanted to admit him. But John wanted to get back to Greenville. We arranged to have him taken by ambulance to the Greenville hospital. Vic and Janet left for their home, and I set out for Greenville. It was almost 11 p.m. Not seeing well and always afraid to drive at night, I was exhausted, worried, and alone. I hated being alone, and yet I was always more so than not. I prayed all the way down the mountain. I told myself forcefully: *You are alone because you chose to be. You made your bed, you lie in it*, as my dad would have said.

But Anne was on the way to Greenville from Columbia. We met John in the Greenville emergency department and waited again for several hours for him to be admitted. Finally at 4 a.m., I went home to collapse for a few hours, and Anne stayed with him in his new room.

Lying in bed, I remembered the previous Tuesday night. I had come upon John standing in his room, staring at his chest of drawers. Realizing he wasn't doing anything, I went up to him and said, "What is it, darling?" and saw that he was crying.

"Something's wrong. I'm not getting well. I worked so hard in rehab, and I'm not getting better. I think it's still the Wegener's."

"Oh, honey, no! There just hasn't been enough time! It's going to be okay."

The memory chilled me. I prayed it was only this intestinal thing and nothing more.

John was horribly sick. It was C. diff (*colostrum difficile*), an intestinal infection that often comes to immuno-compromised patients. He was in terrible pain, unbearable to watch. I called Duke—Dr. Allen's fellow, Dr. George, called me back immediately and wanted John to come back there. But John wasn't willing. A new rheumatologist came in and started him on plasma; his hemoglobin was low again. His kidney function was lower again, too.

That day, the rheumatologist told us that likely the Wegener's was still hiding in his kidneys, never having gone fully into remission. It was too early for any more Rituxan, and with two infections, his body couldn't withstand any more chemotherapy right now anyway. The pulmonologist told us all that he needed to be back at Duke—that if it were her child, she would have him live in Durham for a year.

49

We didn't have the money to do that. No one could leave jobs and live in another place. And John was adamantly resistant to going back to Duke, regardless. Where I saw Duke as the place that saved his life, he viewed it as the place where he almost died.

My knees hurt so bad that I could hardly walk. All the walking in bad shoes at Duke finally triggered arthritis. It was a challenge to make it to work and then to walk the seeming miles at the Greenville hospital in the evenings to see John. I visited an orthopedist who recommended physical therapy, but I didn't have time and opted for cortisone shots instead. He also started me on a prescription anti-inflammatory medication.

John came back home on August 30, this time with a walker. Anne and I had a hard time getting him in; he fell going up the front steps. He was to go back to Duke for a follow-up clinic visit, and I had told Vic I couldn't take him. I was still having trouble walking, and I couldn't physically support John. Vic said he would come and take him, and Anne would go, too. They would need to get a wheel chair for him at the Millennium and at the Duke clinic.

Megan called that night to say that she was pregnant. Though it was a really good thing—she and Haynes had been married three years and would be wonderful parents—all I could feel was overwhelmed. I so wanted to be happy and excited about this, my first grandchild, but all my energy was taken with trying to keep my other child alive.

Allison—September 2, Year One

Two days later, a Wednesday, John went to Duke. The clinic visits took until late in the day, so they stayed at the Millennium that night. He and Anne were back at my house by late afternoon Thursday. He was tired and weak and had trouble getting off the sofa when he wanted to take a bath. A co-worker of mine had installed a tub rail, and the husband of another had put up a ramp at our front porch. We grilled out hotdogs and later marshmallows, and John and Anne watched the USC football game. The next day Anne went to Charleston for the Labor Day weekend.

Since the recent hospitalization, John had to check his blood sugar for steroid-induced diabetes. By Friday, he was almost too weak to move and his sugar was high. Dr. George called from Duke; the Greenville nephrology office was also calling, having received the report on the labs done at Duke on Wednesday. Dr. George was also concerned that the fluid he was retaining could affect his breathing and wanted him to have labs rechecked and a 24-hour urinalysis done. But it was after 4 on Friday afternoon, the start of the Labor Day weekend, and everything was closed.

The prescription John had been given for insulin was not the pen-injection type he had been trained on at the hospital but rather the old-fashioned type that had to be drawn up in a syringe. I knew neither of us could do this. I called my friends Roger and Ellen; Roger was a doctor. They came over and Roger instructed me in drawing up a syringe; John gave himself a shot. Fearing I would draw up the wrong amount and kill him, this still ranked as one of the most frightening things I had to do.

On Saturday, John was too sick to get out of bed and had not voided in almost 24 hours. Doctors were telling me to get him to the hospital, but he refused to let me call an ambulance. Finally, by afternoon, I called my friends again. Roger and Ellen, both tall and strong, managed to get John up and, one under each of his arms, into my car. I drove to the Greenville emergency door and pushed the button for help. Immediately John was taken in, in complete kidney failure, and admitted to the renal floor where he was to start dialysis.

John—End Stage Renal Disease, September, Year One

Being on paralytics during the induced coma left me incredibly weak. Most of the muscle mass I had gained in a quarter of a century seemed to melt away overnight. I wasn't ever "big" or anything, but I played every sport I could since I was three or four. I rarely played with action figures or "toys" growing up but rather had a soccer ball at my feet pretty much any time I wasn't in school. That included banging it up and down the stairs of the three-story house I spent my childhood in and spending hours before, during, and after soccer practice learning how to curve the ball and basically make it go anywhere I wanted it to. I scored goals on occasion but kept my spot at center midfield on my club team for my ability to distribute the ball. Knowing where my teammates were and how to get the ball to them while both running full speed with defenders and without ever missing a stride was why I loved to play. Of course, goals are cool, too. But if I thought anyone on my team had a better angle or more skill scoring, I'd pass it every time. The ability to know every strength and weakness of every one of my teammates (including myself) and know what they'd likely do in any given situation (on and off the field) was the best part of being on a soccer team.

The best part of football was locker room shenanigans. My favorite part of baseball was the dugout, bean balls, and post-game brawls. Wrestling and track built comradery through the pain, sweat, and tears you go through together, as well as the desire for your teammates to do great—as long as they didn't do as great as you!

Having strong thighs and calves was somewhat of a badge of honor in the soccer community and didn't hurt when I ran varsity track in seventh and eighth grades, played church league basketball, Little League baseball, varsity wrestling, and served several years as the place kicker for my high school football team. Now, looking down and not being able to notice any difference while flexing my calves in the hospital bed was something I hated. Like Forrest Gump, I had relied on my legs through the good and the bad. (Like when high school parties got busted by the police and you need to hurdle a few fences to keep from getting a ticket for underage possession of alcohol. Or when you and a buddy decide to "park bench" your rival's quarterback outside of a bar in Columbia.)

I knew I could get my legs back. I worked as hard to walk—specifically walk up stairs —as much as I have worked at anything. Being physically incapable of getting myself on and off of the toilet wasn't something I was willing to live with for long. My family was happy to see me up and working and scared to death that I was working too hard or would collapse at any time. And I did take some falls. Thinking I could pull one leg up the five-to-six inches of one stair as easily as before led to some embarrassing and discouraging spills.

I was mad at myself for not paying more attention, mad at my body for not doing what in my sports days wouldn't take more thought than blinking, and mad at anyone around me for seeing me in such a weak state. I felt twice as bad when these stairs or curbs got the best of me in front of my family or girlfriend. I wanted to be strong for them even more than for myself.

At times, the fear of Wegener's was debilitating. The thought of relapse would hit suddenly, bringing panic, tears, and shaking.

And things weren't getting better. Within a few weeks of leaving Roger C. Peace, I was unable to move from my mom's living room couch. My kidneys were no longer functioning.

Allison—September 16, Year one

I had just come into John's room on the nephrology wing. Anne was there, and they were both perturbed by the usual lack of communication and agreement among the members of the nephrology group. As I was trying to discern what was being said, John handed me a booklet and said, "Somebody left this. She said we are supposed to go to a class or something."

The label on the front of the folder said "New to Renal Group Information." I opened it to find stapled pages and brochures describing End Stage Renal Disease. There was also one titled, "Five Wishes," referring to end-of-life choices. Before I could make myself finish the first paragraph, I closed it, got up, and said, "I'm going to find the nurse."

At the busy station, I waited to catch someone's attention. Finally I asked, holding out the book, "There's a class I'm supposed to go to about this?" My hand was shaking and my voice trembled a bit.

I was told that the class was over but that someone would come find me and explain more. I went back to the room and tried to learn more about what the doctor said, but John wasn't talking. Anne said that the doctors didn't know what they were doing. Then the person came to talk to me and suggested we go to a conference room down the hall.

What I knew when I read the first sentence—maybe what didn't connect with 26-year-olds—was that "end-stage" anything was not good. Terror filled me anew. I was hoping I was over-reacting, as I seem often to be accused of. I was not.

The nurse explained that John's kidneys were non-functioning and would not regain function, and that the only way he could live was to stay on dialysis for the rest of his life or until he had a successful kidney transplant. I tried to tell her what happened at Duke, what he'd been through, that he'd been on dialysis before and was able to come off it . . . . She looked at me with sympathy and said, "It's always hard when an acute illness becomes chronic." I didn't hear much beyond that point. John didn't die; he was healed; he was supposed to be all right! Then Labor Day weekend, he had gone into complete kidney failure.

John and Anne looked up as I came back in, John studying my face. I kept my eyes averted. "I'm going to leave for a while; I'll bring you back some supper. Text me what you want." I knew they could tell I was crying.

The next day, John had another kidney biopsy. The report was that seven out of nine glomeruli in both kidneys were irrevocably destroyed by the Wegener's. The other two were crescent-shaped, indicating acute, aggressive injury. The nephrologists were "on the fence" as to whether "acutely active Wegener's" was present. Again I begged to go back to Duke. Again John, along with Anne, refused. The doctor did not want to give more Cytoxan, since it had such dangerous side effects and it hadn't seemed to help much earlier in John's disease progression. The Rituxan, which had saved his lungs (and life) in July couldn't be given sooner than four-to-six months.

"Get him up here!" Dr. George insisted. "We'll figure it out," and I believe that Duke would have, after seeing them work this summer.

But the nephrologists felt there was really "nothing to salvage" and began discussing surgery for the creation of a graft or fistula for dialysis access. Vascular surgeons were called in. Nobody else seemed to be concerned about the Wegener's possibly still being active.

On September 21, John had the first of several unsuccessful attempts to get a working fistula. This one clotted off while he was still in Recovery. Surgery was again scheduled for the next day. He woke in terrible pain in Recovery; the attending physician had left for the day, and the resident couldn't prescribe any more pain medication. I went into action and cited the Lewis Blackman Act, which mandated that an attending be called when a patient or family requested it, in order to get an attending physician called back in to get John additional pain medication. This time the graft clotted off in two weeks. The central line, put in at Duke in July, had to continue to be used for dialysis access. The nephrologists said that "since good access is not happening, disproportionate weight is placed on transplant."

John came home on September 29, after nearly another month hospitalized.

John—Good Days, Fall, Year One

My time in hospitals was split with two months in Greenville, two months at Duke, and then the better part of the next four months back at Greenville. It's strange to say, but it wasn't always terrible. For one thing, I had zero responsibilities. It was the first time since I was 16 that I didn't have a job to worry about. Insurance was covering almost all the hospital bills, so for the first time since I was a kid, I really didn't have to worry about money. It was a strange feeling and one that took a while to set in. In the beginning I was anxious about how much it all would cost. I tried not to ask for bandages, tape, or anything I thought would increase my bill. My mom finally told me to quit worrying about it and just try to get better. After that I finally asked for a new pair of bright yellow safety socks, or "Big Bird" socks as we called them.

My family and Anne were there and friends would visit. I was eventually given the right combo of meds to be comfortable enough to sleep and relax. My days consisted of waking up around 4:30-5:00 in the morning when doctors would do their rounds. They might make some small changes in medications, but I'd usually get a few more hours of sleep until the nurses' shift change. With that I would get vitals read, turn the TV on, and sit up in bed. Shortly after that, Anne would bring me a breakfast sandwich she made in the cafeteria and we'd eat together. Depending on the day I could have an MRI, CT, X-ray, or some other small procedure that would get me out of the room for a few hours. Depending on my condition, I'd be taken to these in a wheelchair or in my bed. The transporters were always friendly and down to earth. We'd talk on the ride only to be interrupted by them saying, "Bump," every time we rolled over a door jam or into an elevator. I'm sure it's something they have to say, and it is a nice heads-up when you are in serious pain, but most of the time it would make me chuckle hearing it over and over every day.

A schoolmate and football teammate from high school was a medical student there, so he'd stop by and shoot the shit with me. It was nice to have a friend aware of how sick I was but who didn't look at me like a leper. He could also answer questions that my family or I had when we couldn't get hold of a specific doctor.

Nice nurses were a real benefit. I could tell the moment he or she walked into the room what my next twelve hours would be like. Bad nurses can make your day hell.

My favorite nurse at Duke was Zeliah. She reminded me of Smith's ex-girlfriend. I remember her having a dry sense of humor and not really caring whether my family or I liked her. I thought she worked nights, but now I'm thinking that may be wrong because there weren't many night nurses I liked. I was told many months later that she was the one who would hook a basin to my bed and wash my hair, even French-braided it once. I remember my family not being very fond of her. Mom said that was true until they realized how well she worked with me.

I wish I could thank her, along with many other doctors and nurses who were so critical at one point or another and whom I may never see again.

Allison—October, Year One

Unless you've had the experience of long-term hospital stays, there is really no way to know what it is like. Whether you are there as a patient or even a family member, the time is grueling. It's nothing like working there, when you can leave when your shift is done or the crisis is over. Even today, entering the Greenville hospital by the Rehab entrance, as I watch family members visiting with their patients in wheelchairs in the outdoor courtyard, I see other times.

Today I was here only to pick up my own prescription at the hospital pharmacy. I walked through the food court and images flashed by me – of John walking to Chick-fil-A, dragging his IV pole, sleeve cut out of his T-shirt . . . immediate family gathered around a cafeteria table on a Saturday after we'd been asked to leave the ICU . . . countless evenings of standing in line to get food to take up to his room . . . . There was remembered terror in the multitude of scenes, the seeming unending repetition of fear and exhaustion.

Incredibly, each hospitalization was totally new to the staff, as if John had never been there before. Interns, residents, and physicians asked the same questions over and over, with seemingly no information communicated. John had learned to halt every clinician at his bedside or in the operating room to remind him or her of his heparin reaction; any product containing it was life threatening to him. Probably 40 times a day he repeated his date of birth in response to their question. He frequently reminded them "No sticks" in his right arm, where vascular surgeons were trying to preserve a useful vein. I finally did a four-page summary of his conditions and hung it in plastic sheet protectors from his IV pole. The lack of communication was appalling.

With every hospitalization, John's immediate goal was always to *get out*. He had little control over anything but perhaps what he could eat, so he gave us his orders for carryout and even had pizza delivered once when he was at Duke by himself. Most of the time he was tethered to a bed by an IV line. Techs came in at random hours during the night, turning on the overhead lights and calling loudly. Residents started their rounds at 4 a.m.

with attending physicians coming in before seven. His cell phone was his connection to life, and he managed to hide it and even carry it into surgery on more than one occasion.

With each subsequent hospitalization, he came home with a leftover box of Glad Press'n Seal. Every time he took a shower—for almost two years—he had to carefully "seal" his subclavian port with plastic wrap, to prevent infection in his chest cavity. Still today, I almost recoil when I open a drawer and see Press'n Seal resting beside the Saran Wrap.

Also with each hospitalization, because of the blood clots and the need to be on Coumaden, he had to be transitioned off this blood thinner by an intravenous medication (Argatroban). This process necessitated a couple of extra days of hospitalization before any surgical procedure—which otherwise potentially could have been done as outpatient—and then about four days on the back end, transitioning back onto oral Coumaden. These were excruciating days of boredom, with labs drawn every few hours and waiting only on numbers to change. I think he watched every movie ever made and got a good start on reading nearly every book. More than once he'd threatened to leave against medical advice (AMA), and twice the doctors had given in and let him go.

This stay, he was determined to be out of the hospital by October 2. It was his twenty-seventh birthday and he made it that day, as he intended, to Atlanta for the Braves game with Anne, Megan and Haynes. I didn't think he was well enough to go, but nothing was stopping him.

John—Fall, Year One

Megan and I were very lucky to have a babysitter named Edna growing up. Both our parents worked, so Edna was a big part of our childhood. She folded clothes and did a few things around the house while she kept us after school. Edna never learned how to drive a car, so occasionally we would get picked up from kindergarten or elementary school in a Yellow Cab. Which officially made her the best babysitter ever, in my opinion. I got to ride in the front seat and was probably the only kid in town every cabbie knew by name. I couldn't wait until I was big enough to drive with my hand gripping the roof and my elbow on the door the way those guys did.

We loved Edna and thought she was the funniest person alive. And she may be. If we acted up she would threaten to sit on us, which we thought was equally scary as hilarious. (She was not a small person.) Edna also warned us to stay out of trouble because they served dog food in prison.

While I can't speak for prison, I've had the displeasure of a meal or three in jail. Nothing serious. The usual underage drinking or fighting, and then being scared (or smart) enough to wait it out rather than call my parents. While I wasn't given dog food, at least not anything I'd feed my dog, I'd wager they use the same recipe for grits at the jails I (briefly) visited as they did at the Citadel Summer Camp where I spent three weeks during most summers of my adolescence. Breakfast was always worth attending (it was also mandatory) at camp just to see how long the grits could stay in an upside down serving dish without falling out (which was eternity). The scrambled eggs were the opposite, being so watery they'd slide right off your plate, so I tried to fill up on burnt bacon every morning. If you didn't inherit the taste for burnt bacon from your uncle, like I did, you could fight for cereal or choke down the eggs and grits.

All this is to say, I would rather eat prison-house dog food and Citadel camp grit-bricks and watery eggs for a year than take one bite of the form-pressed stuff they call food in the hospital CCU. I don't know what it actually is—some kind of protein mix, maybe? The bright yellow, half-ear of fake corn will never leave my memory. And by half I mean that it was flat on one side and molded to look like it had kernels on the other. Whatever it was, it wasn't corn. Luckily, I was still so doped up at this particular meal that I tried eating with the convex side of a spoon, so I doubt much made it farther than my lap.

It's only fair to say that some hospitals have better food and more options than others, and if all else fails, get your friends and family to bring in as many meals as possible. (Or ask if there's a secret menu! One actually existed at Duke and may have kept me from going insane from the monotony of the regular options.)

There were times when the doctors would crack down and remind me that I was on a diet of no sugar (steroid induced diabetes), no sodium (kidney function and water retention so bad I could've passed for Elephant Man), no leafy green veggies (blood thinners), no cranberry or grapefruit (can't remember which medication that interacted with), no whole grain, no fresh fruit . . . .

After stopping the fourth dietician/nutritionist from spouting off the list of things I couldn't eat and receiving stumped silence when I asked to list some possible meals I could eat, I went back to take-out.

Allison—October 21, Year One

John was back in the hospital again, third time here since leaving Duke—this time with pleural effusion, or fluid in the lung. He was on IV antibiotics again. He was released after a week and then the following day readmitted, with a blood clot in his lung. This time I called EMS and then we spent hours in the critical care part of the Emergency department with no one attending to him. He was in terrible pain, and I was beside myself. I finally saw one of his pulmonologists and accosted him.

"Please come help him!" I begged.

My action caused the nurse manager to be summoned. She came to calm me down, to explain the delay. Instead, I broke down, spitting out, "I don't care about what is going on with the other patients! Do something for *him!*" I was crying now; the strain of watching him suffer was too much.

I was angry that he was released and then readmitted in such critical shape in less than 24 hours, and that no one seemed to care. Again I asked that he be transferred to Duke, but the pulmonologists felt there was no critical need that warranted transfer.

John stayed almost two weeks this time, coming home on November 10. Following that, he struggled with another bout of C. diff that we managed at home, with dialysis, and with Coumaden clinic. Days were bleak. The single toilet clogged and there was some type of creature in the interior wall of my house. Nights, I got up to help John change sheets, beat against the wall at the scratching noise, and thought that we would never hear from Medicare (which he was eligible for since the diagnosis of End Stage Renal Disease). We were waiting on outpatient appointments at Duke, but they weren't scheduled for another month.

This was too hard. It was all too hard. I was alone with the incredible responsibility of helping John live, in every way. There was no one to help. I felt I would never live through this myself.

Allison—November 11, Year One

I was driving today to Charleston for a few days to attend the annual professional conference that I had gone to for years. I was so glad for a break and to be going to my favorite place. I had tentatively asked Tom to meet me there, but I was glad when he didn't. The strain of a long-distance relationship, along with his continued joblessness as a result of the recession plus John's illness, had not been easy.

About thirty miles from Charleston, Anne called to say John had been taken by ambulance from dialysis to the Emergency room; he was unresponsive and then confused. I called Megan in Atlanta and asked if she could go and meet Anne, so that she wouldn't have to be alone. They didn't admit him, couldn't really find anything wrong. Megan stayed, and the next day it was a repeat—taking him back to the ER from dialysis, doctors not knowing what was wrong, and not admitting . . . . Anne and I made a pact that if he needed to go to the ER again, we were driving him straight to Duke. I was desperate to get him back there.

Allison—December 6, Year One

Cold rain as again I drove John to Baptist Easley Hospital. His doctor had recommended a brain scan and that we take it with us to the Duke appointments on the 8. John slept almost the whole time, what he had been doing most of the time the past couple of weeks. We walked down the corridor decorated for the Festival of Trees, but my heart was far from festive.

The MRI showed a questionable area on his brain. My sense of foreboding was reinforced. I prayed that the Wegener's would not take him from us.

Wednesday morning I got up early to ready us to leave for Duke. I stayed on my knees for a while and prayed in near desperation. I didn't know what to do. He hadn't been able to take his medications correctly by himself, and sometimes he barely seemed functional. I was afraid we wouldn't be able to care for him at home, that he would have to go to an assisted living facility. I couldn't feel any hope or see any positive end. The responsibility for trying to keep him alive was heavier than I could bear. I didn't know what to do but go on to Duke.

John slept in the back seat; Anne drove. We were going to see Dr. Perfect, the Infectious Diseases specialist. He treated John in the summer and was the best in the world, literally, in the treatment of cryptococcus, the yeast infection that infiltrated John's lungs and spinal fluid last summer.

The appointment was at 2 p.m. Anne and I took him back in a wheel chair. I had the CD with the brain scan on it. Dr. Perfect, which was literally his name and who looked so not-perfect but rather like Cromagnon Man, viewed it and then said, "I'll be back. I'm going to get this to the radiologist."

He returned and then said, "I want to admit him. Hang out here until I get through seeing patients and then I'll take you over myself."

All I could feel was overwhelming relief. John slept as we waited, occasionally involuntarily nearly jerking himself off the exam table. At almost 5 p.m., Dr. Perfect came back, and true to his word, walked us over to Duke hospital through the construction breezeway where I'd walked so often in the summer. Now it was frigid with leftover snow on the ground and tops of buildings. Anne pushed John in the wheelchair. Dr. Perfect walked us straight into Admitting, talked to the representative, and did the paperwork on the spot to get him admitted. Then he walked us upstairs to John's newly assigned room.

Memories flashed by me: the wall of elevators I'd waited in front of so often. The windowed atrium on the eighth floor where I'd paced for hours. The distinctive smell of the soap in the bathroom; the green toilet handle that pulls up to flush for one and down for two. I saw one of the residents from the summer who remembered and hugged me. This time there was a large Christmas tree in the courtyard.

As we walked, Dr. Perfect talked of his suspicions: that the cryptococcal infection was in John's brain, that he wanted to get a spinal tap immediately. Dr. Perfect did a thorough hand-off of information himself to John's nurse. I asked that Rheumatology also be called; Dr. George responded quickly, too. By the next day we had learned that it was not infection but most likely Wegener's activity in the brain, a place the disease rarely attacks. They would start a second round of Rituxan, the treatment that saved his lungs in July.

Allison—December 9, Year One

Anne and I left the next day, not having come prepared to stay, and Vic and Janet drove up to be with John. They only stayed through the weekend, leaving John in intense pain. John texted me the next day, begging to come home. I told him to hang on, that Megan was on her way and would be there later that day. She was taking Christmas lights to decorate his room.

The following day, December 15 and Megan's birthday, John was yelling and throwing things at the Pain Management doctors. Megan left his room in tears, alone and pregnant on her thirtieth birthday. I was torn, that both my kids were hurting and away from me. Still, I trusted the doctors at

SINCE JOHN GOT SICK

Duke and was glad he was there. Heavy snow was predicted for that night and the next day.

Megan drove John home the following day. The doctors didn't think he was ready to leave but couldn't hold him. It was snowing as they drove; I prayed constantly for their safety. It was a rough few days but slowly John was more positive. The steroids were still keeping him keyed up, but the pain was better. Megan stayed, and we shopped for Christmas.

Allison—December 24, Year One

In keeping with tradition, we all—John, Anne, Megan, Haynes, and I—went to the service at First Baptist and then to the Gowers on Christmas Eve. It was a happy time and I got a picture taken of us for a New Year's letter, since the annual Christmas card had passed me by. We were all glad that 2010 was ending; John had spent most of the past eight months in hospitals.

As usual, that night we each opened one present. Mine was a pink card with an ultrasound photo. My first grandchild would be a girl.

I wanted to be happy, but the shock of all that had happened and my fear for John overrode everything.

4

Transplant

Allison—Winter, Year One

MY CAT SUDDENLY ATTACKED my hand while I was trying to pull up the afghan. I hurried to the kitchen sink, blood starting to drip. I was already thinking, *I'm glad this is me and not John*, when I saw blood rivers down the side of the sink.

Immediately, my mind flashed to another scene: it was as if John were standing there. I remembered when he'd just come in from dialysis and started to remove the bandage, and suddenly blood was spurting. He applied pressure and put his arm under a stream of cold water. There was blood on his white T-shirt, the white sink, the checkerboard floor. I was stunned and then panicked; he was calm. Finally it slowed and I helped him bandage it. Exhausted, he went to his room and to bed, too tired to eat supper.

The next day, the dialysis nurse cautioned him. "Be careful that doesn't happen when you're asleep. You could bleed out and never know it."

That's what dialysis was like. That, or the days when they couldn't get access at all and he came in full of large-needle sticks, with bloodstained shirt, and no dialysis. "Come back tomorrow and we'll try again," was the message.

The centers themselves had rows of recliners where plastic tubing hooked patients' veins to machines for several hours. Blood was removed from their bodies and then put back in. It was an exhausting, medieval-looking process. Many of the patients came and went by ambulance, all dependent on dialysis to live. Some had limbs removed. John's favorite patient was a man with no legs and no teeth who'd been coming for nearly 30 years and who was always inexplicably happy.

Ever since the heparin-induced thrombosis (HIT) early on, John was on blood thinners to keep more clots from forming. He'd had four clots including one in his lung. He'd had vascular surgeries, too, to get adequate access for dialysis. Surgeons would need multiple attempts to make a working fistula—that was, to graft a vein to an artery. One arm had a vicious scar from his elbow to his armpit. This was where the last attempt was; he was waiting for it to "mature" to be of use. There was also a scar on that arm near his wrist—a second failed attempt—and some permanent loss of feeling there. His other upper arm showed the outline of a plastic piece, a graft—the first effort, that failed initially within 48 hours and then again in the recovery room after a re-do attempt. For most of these months, they'd had to keep using the catheter under his collarbone, until it got blocked and seriously infected.

I watched him get up and go three days a week to the dialysis center for too many months.

John—Dialysis, Winter, Year One

Dialysis was truly amazing. I knew almost nothing about it before it was essential for my survival. The most frustrating thing is to hear someone say they would rather die than go on dialysis. Although for me it was something to keep my body working until I could find a donor, many people are on dialysis for years. Toward the end of the 20 or so months I was on dialysis, a man at my center "celebrated" 30 years of dialysis. While it's difficult to imagine the suffering this man has been through, you also have to see what a blessing these 30 years have been. He had been through two or three transplants by this point and probably didn't want another one even if he had the chance.

I think it's easy for someone to say they would never live a certain way until they're actually faced with it. This man, Jimmy, had the best sense of humor at the clinic and still worked as a barber. His favorite show was "Family Feud" and several men would change their personal TV's hanging in front of them to that channel midway through our four-hour session at 6 p.m. These guys would yell out answers and comments to each other, so from time to time, I would turn it on to be in on the joke. I only remember one of his answers, and we laughed about it many times after.

A little over a year after my transplant I started driving patients to and from dialysis for an ambulance service. The time I happened to pick up Jimmy, I was sad to see that he'd had to have a foot amputated (as do so many patients with diabetes). We all had a good laugh when I repeated

Steve Harvey's line, "We surveyed 100 people, top five answers are on the board. Name a way to get your wife to stop complaining," to the EMT riding in the back getting vitals, and Jimmy answered, "Punch her in her throat!" just as he had one night a couple years earlier while we were sitting beside each other at dialysis. I'll be back on dialysis at some point. Depending on how long I live and how many transplants I survive, I could be on and off dialysis multiple times. It's a pretty shitty thought, but I have some solace knowing that people like Jimmy and the nurse that stuck me every single time will be there in good spirits.

Allison—January—May, Year One

The new year began with dark and uneventful days of John going to dialysis and back to Duke for the second half of the rituximab chemo infusion, Anne to her volunteer job, and me to my job in Easley. Those days were broken only by John Greene Week and a snowstorm, six inches. I wondered how John would get to dialysis, but he made it in the truck, slipping and sliding. I didn't know how he did it—except that he wanted to live. And this was the only way, for now.

Organized by his friends with daily activities plus T-shirt and wrist-band sales, John Greene Week began the initial seed money for John's hope for transplant. His friends had always meant so much to him, and seeing them rally around him was more valuable than money to him.

By mid-February, John had two more infections, another visit to the Duke nephrologists, and the third vascular surgery attempt in Greenville. This one was done in the wrist area of his right hand and might possibly work. Then it was back to Duke for a rheumatology visit, where he started on another form of oral chemo. Dr. George and Dr. Allen told him how well he was doing, that less than a year ago he almost died, that his was the worst case of Wegener's that Duke had ever seen. A few days later, February 22, he learned at dialysis the wrist fistula was "dead." He also had a major conflict with Anne and she moved to a friend's house. Those late February days were as depressing as they were dark.

Yet somehow I was feeling the ground beneath me, finally. I was there for him– and I knew that he knew it.

March 17, I was in the kitchen area at work, getting coffee. My co-worker came in to say, "I wanted to make sure you knew. April's mother died last night." She caught me as I swayed against the counter. "Wha-at?" I stammered.

Shortly after John had gone to Duke last summer, I learned that another hospital employee's relative had been recently diagnosed with Wegener's and hospitalized in Greenville. This woman's case hadn't seemed too bad; I had been envious when I heard she was released to home after a few weeks. What I didn't know was that she had other medical conditions and had chosen not to fight, not to go onto dialysis, and that hospice had been called in. Now she was gone, and John still fought on. I was so glad to see his bright eyes every morning when I went in to check on him and tell him goodbye.

A couple of days later, we went to Duke for John to see a vascular surgeon. A venogram, or vein mapping, was scheduled for the end of the month, the day before the scheduled visit to the Duke Transplant Center.

Then he was sick again. He'd been in bed a week on the last Saturday in the month, when there was a baby shower for Megan in Spartanburg. It was raining, and I was so worried about John, I was present for her only in body. By Monday, he was still too sick to go to dialysis, so I got him to the doctor. The doctor wanted to hospitalize him, do stool studies, start him on IV antibiotics, get Infectious Diseases involved. John refused, saying, "That appointment Thursday for the transplant evaluation is the most important one of my life."

Two days later, I drove him back to Duke. It was a hard drive, heavy rain all the way. John slept. Last night we learned that Vic couldn't be a donor, because of a pre-existing condition. Megan couldn't either, until she was through her childbearing years. All three of them—John, Vic, Megan—were Type A; I was the different one, with Type O. I had not even considered being a donor. But I learned that, as with blood donation, Type O is universal donor for organs. I couldn't stand for John to be let down, so I called and passed the initial screening by phone as I waited for him in the Cath Lab waiting area. I was tired, tired of John being sick, of the day-to-day responsibility while working and trying to keep up the house and yard and finances, mostly tired of being alone in the responsibility of his care. But I was glad that I was healthy, except for my knees. I knew that people were praying for me. Even with the overwhelming load and now the shifting in possible donor status, I felt stronger. Or at least tougher.

The vascular surgeon had good news. He would graft a fistula deep in John's right arm. Surgery was scheduled for week after next. It would be two to four weeks before it could be used. Then in a few months, he would do another surgery to lift the fistula closer to the surface. For now, dialysis would continue to be done through John's chest catheter.

We returned to the Millennium Hotel before the next day's visit to the Transplant Center. That day, March 31, Vic and Janet met us there. In the morning seminar, we learned that John would need two caregivers (primary and secondary), that he would need to spend at least a month in Durham after the hospitalization, that he would have to take anti-rejection meds for the rest of his life, and that these were ridiculously expensive. The biggest reason for rejection was that people couldn't afford their medications and thus stopped taking them; we were encouraged to begin fundraising. Medicare would pay for most of the costs of the transplant, for both recipient and donor. The team stressed that transplant was not a cure but rather an alternative to dialysis. I was told that I could not be both a donor and caregiver, and that he would have to have another caregiver if I were to be the donor. No one stepped forward.

After lunch, we all met with a social worker and then a financial counselor. John would need a secondary insurance or $30,000 in savings to begin the process; thank goodness we were still paying COBRA.

Then the nephrologist examined John and later called us to come in also. He wanted John to be without hospitalizations (except for scheduled vascular surgeries) and have a period of stability for six to eight months, to have a complete work-up with hematology and also particularly with cardiology. When I said, quoting the previous cardiologist, "He has the heart of an athlete; his heart is fine," this doctor told me that was before months on a ventilator, kidney failure, and dialysis. He reminded us that John had an aggressive, unusual case of Wegener's, and that "transplant has not been studied in this complex a patient."

"Time will tell," he said. "Let's see what the tests show. We don't want to rush into anything."

John was scheduled to return in June. I, too, would be tested at his return visit. Not exactly the day, the outcome, he'd hoped for. It was a quiet drive home.

Back home, John had dialysis two days in a row and was exhausted, feet cramping painfully. He went straight to bed. I hated it when he was ill and there was nothing I could do. I folded his laundry. I thought about Dr. Jolly telling us when she discharged him last August that he would be fine; she was very wrong. Then I prayed for forgiveness for my lack of faith in

John's healing. My older friend and prayer warrior, Elizabeth, had never wavered in her belief that John would come through this and be fine.

I remembered that John was our "Blue Intruder," that he wanted to be born. In 1983, I was taking a drawing class in Louisville three days a week before work. Megan was two and Vic was in graduate school when I found out I was pregnant. My art instructor had just given us the assignment "Blue Intruder," to be interpreted however we chose. So I drew John, *in utero*, in shades of blue pastels, and won Honorable Mention. He was our "gift of God," the meaning of the name we chose for him.

On April 8, John left for the vascular surgery at Duke. Anne, still in and out of the picture, had offered to take him and stay Friday through Sunday. Tom, also, had been more out of the picture than in. The situation was just too hard.

The surgery went well and John returned home. Soon after, Anne moved on, taking a job in Columbia and going on with the rest of her life. I didn't know the why of all that. But I was grateful she was in our lives for that difficult year. Megan and Haynes moved from Atlanta to Tennessee, five hours away. John and I kept our vigil alone.

Megan's due date was early May, and John and I were committed to being there. He spent hours working with social workers and getting forms signed to be able to get dialysis in some remote part of Tennessee. The closest center to Megan's home in Sewanee was thirty miles away, in the small town of Winchester. She was having the baby in Chattanooga, an hour the other way.

We left Greenville the morning of May 8 and arrived ahead of Millie on that Mother's Day. For the second year in a row, I celebrated Mother's Day with one or the other of my children in a hospital bed—but at least this time was a happy one.

I was grateful for the new life that had entered our families, but I was never too far from the worry over John. He was exhausted that night on the dark drive from Chattanooga to Sewanee.

Early the next day, he and I located the small dialysis center that helped keep him alive the week we were in Tennessee.

John—Doctors and Limits, Spring, Year Two

There was a limit to how much doctors could get away with, and one day I found mine.

After three failed local surgeries, I returned to Duke to have a fistula put in for dialysis. A fistula is the safer and more permanent option for hemodialysis access. The other option is a catheter. (There are also internal port devices that I didn't know about at the time.) This type of catheter is usually inserted through the neck, into the jugular vein, and guided to the heart. The exterior end is tunneled through a skin "cuff," and two tubes are left to dangle on your chest. Because there is always an opening in the skin and because the catheter goes directly to the heart, it is vital to keep it covered, cleaned, and out of the water. Of course this entails no swimming or bathing and paying close attention while showering. It's generally a huge pain in the ass but it's keeping you alive, so you get used to it.

Luckily the fistula surgery at Duke incurred no clots and was success-ful. It was also terrible! It lasted several hours longer than expected, took 40 staples to close, and was some of the worst pain I remember. In the recov-ery room I asked the nurse for more pain medicine and remember being told that the anesthesiologist on duty was "upstairs sleeping" and couldn't come. After hours later of wishing I was dead, I received two milligrams of Dilaudid through my IV. Having been on large amounts of painkillers for at least a year for considerably less pain, this dosage barely did anything. There were times when I had been given four mgs of IV Dilaudid every eight hours on top of the Fentanyl patch and multiple oral pain meds I received daily. It eventually stopped hurting, and I was able to head back to Greenville once I got put back on my oral blood thinner (Coumadin) and off IV Argatroban.

The new fistula was in use shortly after returning home and the cath-eter could finally come out. This would be the first time in at least a year that my body wouldn't have some kind of non-biological hole! Catheters usually come out with general ease compared to most procedures—though maybe ease isn't the word. All it usually takes is a sharp tug. I thought it was a joke the first time a doctor came in and told me he was just going to pull them right out of my chest. But he did! It isn't an easy sensation to describe. It usually felt like a small pop somewhere inside my chest and then a cold, wet feeling as they pulled the feet of bloody tubes out.

This time was different and could've landed me in jail. At my appoint-ment at the local nephrologists' office, I was called back shortly after filling out the obligatory paperwork. After being told to take my shirt off and sit back, the doc explained that he was going to try to pull it out without making any incisions. I hesitantly nodded in agreement. Having been through this multiple times before, I knew there was a possibility some skin could've grown around parts of the tube depending on how long it had been in, and making it almost impossible to remove without some minor knife work.

I braced and he tugged. Nothing. Try after try. It took long enough that his nurse answered a phone call and began relaying the caller and the doctor back and forth to each other. All while both his hands are trying to pull a catheter out of my chest/neck/heart!

With clenched fists and thoughts of knocking this doctor flat, I tried asking, as calmly as possible, if he could hold the call for later and focus on the job literally at hand. He was baffled. Before telling me I had no place to tell him what to do and that the call was an emergency, his jaw dropped and he stared at me in shock. And because I could hear both sides of the conversation, I knew it was nothing close to being more of an emergency than the job he was currently doing. It was a patient calling to ask if he should take his blood thinner the morning of surgery. I could've answered the man in two words: "No, moron." Apparently my willingness to confront him was enough for him to bring out the scalpel and cut the necessary tissue away from the chest catheter, something I had suggested after the fourth unsuccessful yank. Thankfully, I never had such issues with Foley catheter extractions!

In fact, the first time I had a Foley removed, I asked nurse Scott if it would hurt; he told me he didn't know because this was his first time to do it.

Allison—Summer, Year Two

On June 23, we returned to the Duke Transplant Center. The nephrologist said to John, "You look better. That's good. I am pleased. It probably means the Wegener's is quiescent and will remain so." The test reports from Cardiology and Hematology had come back good as well. He approved John for the cadaveric transplant list at Duke and explained what that meant.

These kidneys came from deceased persons who had given consent to be organ donors. Donations were granted according to the best match. For example, if someone on the waiting list matches a cadaveric kidney on all six alleles, that person would get it no matter his or her place on the list.

According to the nephrologist, that happens "once in a blue moon" and did occur once in his own career. He concluded, "I am happy with how things are developing," and scheduled John for another check in six months.

Then it was my turn to have blood drawn, despite the unanswered questions of who would be primary caregiver for John (or me). As the older African American lady with gray hair pulled back in a bun drew the sixth vial, I told her I was being tested for my son. She smiled knowingly and said, "Ah. A mother's blood." I was possibly more disturbed than comforted by her words. I didn't see how I could do it.

Stopping by the bathroom before returning to the waiting room, I was aware of strong impressions. There could be another blue moon match. Then as the motion sensors on both hand dryers went off simultaneously, I thought, *Maybe there will be two donors.* I guess I was grasping at straws.

Back in the waiting room with John, I cried for the good news for him, that the report has been positive and that he was now "on the list." When I told Megan by phone, she said my crying was about the timing—where we were this time last year, in the days when we had little hope that John would live. It was amazing, and a little scary, that we could have hope again, that John really might be okay.

In early July, I was variously sick; I resorted to physical therapy for my knees and I also had a lingering sore throat. Then mid-July, John came home in the middle of the night from a weekend visit to Vic's with terrible pain in his arm where the new fistula was "maturing." On Monday, I got an order from the Duke vascular surgeon for John to have a vascular study done at Baptist Easley. He was supposed to go to Duke the following Friday anyway, for the "lifting" of the newly created fistula. The image study showed that there was too much blood flow/pressure backing up into the jugular and thus causing the extreme pain. The Duke surgeon said it would be fine for John to wait and come as scheduled on Friday. As least we knew the cause of the pain.

Then on Wednesday, we got a call from Duke that John's surgery has been bumped and he shouldn't come until Monday. I was incensed and got on the phone to the surgeon's office, but my anger did not change the surgery schedule. John hung on in pain and we drove up on Sunday. Monday was also the day for my all-day evaluation at the Transplant Center. John would go by himself to be admitted and have dialysis that day. I planned to drive back Monday night for necessary meetings. John would be by himself for a few days until Vic could get there.

I learned that I was supposed to have a support person with me for my evaluation, but there was no one. I called the transplant coordinator and she said to come anyway. I had asked my cousin Diane in Florida if she would be my caregiver if I were to be the donor and she had agreed. She would be available by phone on Monday if they wanted to talk to her.

Up and ready to leave for Duke, I my still had a sore throat and was anxious about John's condition, his being alone, my work responsibilities, the possibility of my being a donor, my exhaustion. But I knew that many people were praying for me, for God's will to be done. So I needed only to be in the presence of God and trust.

For the transplant evaluation, I had completed multiple pages of paperwork and knew that I would talk to a donor advocate, a social worker, and a psychologist, as well as undergo an examination by a nephrologist—a different one from John's. I would also have a chest X-ray, ultrasound of my kidneys, and various lab work. That morning I dropped John at Duke Admitting and went to the clinics, 2C.

Throughout the day, John was texting me. The doctor had not left admitting orders, much less an order for dialysis, and was in surgery and couldn't be reached. John was beside himself with pain and frustration. There was nothing I could do. He texted me that he needed me more as a caregiver than as a donor.

At the end of my day, I learned that I was pretty healthy. They had concerns about the medication I was taking for arthritis. I would not be able to take the prescription anti-inflammatory or any NSAID, even ibuprophen. I would need a colonoscopy (since I had not had one at age 50) and be cystoscoped to check bladder function. I was also referred to a psychiatrist to start anti-depression medication. But most importantly, I was a match to John on four alleles.

"You and his father must have a common allele," the doctor told me. "Normally a parent matches on three alleles. This is very good."

But the donor advocate said that I was not a candidate without another caregiver for John, and that at this point, John had been approved only for a cadaveric transplant.

It was after 4:30 p.m. when I was finished, and I hurried over to Duke hospital. John was still sitting in the Admitting waiting room, where he had been pacing, and threatening to leave, all day. After speaking with the

Admitting supervisor, I asked that the patient liaison be called and proceeded to get things moving. Soon John was in a room, admitted by the surgeon's resident. She explained to me that the doctor's pages had been forwarded all day to his cell phone and that the surgical nurse had not thought to answer his cell phone. I really didn't care. I screamed a bit, with the patient advocate present, insisting that the surgeon get up here immediately and that John should have had dialysis today. John lay back in bed, exhausted, glad that I was handling the situation. He never understood how I could always get things done. I knew it was my seven years' experience working as a patient advocate. I was not intimidated by doctors or hospital systems, and I would not tolerate John not being treated adequately.

Soon the vascular surgeon came in. As I was telling him how sick John had been for over a week, that he knew that and should never have postponed his surgery, and now to have ignored him all day . . . . he was examining John and soon began talking over me, urgency in his voice. "This is not good," he said, his eyes and fingers never leaving John's upper arm and chest area. Then he was barking orders. I stepped back and watched the team go into action, thinking that again I had gotten him to Duke's safe place.

I ended up staying that night. The day had been too stressful for both of us. They came for John in the middle of the night to take him to dialysis. Surgery had been moved up and would be on Wednesday.

On Tuesday afternoon, John was calmer, resting, Argatroban drip going in his arm. We now knew that the blockage, or stenosis, was caused by scar tissue from the central catheter being left in his chest for over a year as the only successful means for dialysis. Tomorrow in the surgery, they would remove it, clean out the blockage and put another in its place, and also lift the fistula. I was leaving soon, to get back to work. Vic would be here tomorrow for the surgery. The head resident talked to me, assuring me that John was in good hands, that she herself was studying to be a transplant surgeon. I left to drive the four hours home.

That night John sent me a text: "I can't even write all the things that I am thankful for that you do."

By 10 o'clock Wednesday night, I was certain that John had died. They took him to surgery just after noon. I texted Vic every couple of hours; he said there was no word. I knew that I would have busted through doors to find out what was happening. But I just couldn't be there. Finally at midnight Vic texted that they had let him back to Recovery to see John and he was okay.

Later I learned more details. John's was the last case of the day, and he lay in pre-op for hours with no pain meds. The surgery itself took six hours. He was cut from his elbow to his armpit and also down the midline of his sternum. He was in agony for hours in Recovery with no one paying any attention. Because of the amounts of medication/sedation he had been given for the months while intubated for his various conditions, he required a much higher strength of medication than was normal protocol. Every time we discussed this with the admitting doctor or surgeon, they always said it would not be a problem, and twelve hours later with a different shift, it always was. The good news was that the surgery was successful and the fistula had every chance of working after it healed for a few weeks.

Vic had to leave and John was alone again, tied by IV's to his hospital bed. The Argatroban drip would return his blood consistency to a safe enough level for him to leave on oral Coumaden. His care was now with the hematologists whose job it was to see that nothing clotted off. They were slow and cautious. John was alone and afraid.

Finally it was Wednesday of the following week, final night of the Big League World Series held in Easley and of which Baptist Easley was a major sponsor. Tonight's game would be on ESPN. John should be able to come home in a couple of days, and I had cleared Friday to go get him.

At the ball field, I was helping man our booth, getting our CEO out on the field for first pitch and talking to the media people, when I began getting texts from John. He was desperate, he couldn't stay, I had to come get him. It was 30-45 minutes of intense stress with both knees killing me as I tried to ascertain what was going on with him. "John, I can't come now. Turn on the TV. I am on the field!

"Tell me what it is," I insisted.

Finally he told me that his chest was hurting and he couldn't breathe and he was afraid they would take him to ICU and he would have to go back on the ventilator and he would die.

"You are having a panic attack," I told him. "Let me call someone."

So I reached the nurse and then had the doctor paged, trying to find a quiet and private enough place to hear, as I neglected one responsibility to attend to a more desperate one. I explained what was going on and begged that they do something. The doctor assured me that they would. I relayed this to John.

As soon as I could leave, I called him back. He was calmer. They had gotten the pain management doctor to come in and do some relaxation/

visualization work with him. Just having someone know his fears and pay attention helped relieve the panic. I cancelled the next day's appointments and told him I would be up in the morning.

The next day at Duke, I could see that John was in bad shape emotionally and spiritually. I asked for the chief resident and then the surgeon. With the chief resident, I reminded her that she had told me that I could trust them to take care of him and they had not, that I was disgusted that it took John having a breakdown and my having to drive back up here for anyone to listen and take action. With the surgeon, I thanked him for a successful surgery and told him John needed to leave. He talked with the hematologists who disagreed. John stayed another night, had dialysis the next morning, and then said he was leaving, AMA if necessary. I called the vascular surgeon who said Go!, and discharged him. By afternoon we were back on the road to Greenville.

The good news resulting from this surgery was that the "thrill" was in John's arm. Where an artery now flowed into a vein, there was an almost electric pulsing, a buzzing in John's upper arm. This was what he had waited for in four previous surgeries and what should make dialysis much more effective. The fistula, a vein-artery creation, was now thick and visible, like a half-inch cord bulging under his skin. I was also aware of the danger of an artery that close to the surface, particularly with him on blood thinners.

Soon after this, I seemed to unravel emotionally. I was more depressed. The four-year relationship that I had such hopes for had been more off than on the past year. I was having fears, of my own aging and loss of health, of no more chances for do-overs, that I was out of time in my life, that I would not be able to work and wouldn't have enough money to live, that I was failing at another relationship, for what kind of future John would have. I learned that I was anemic.

John was struggling to figure out his own life, and I was disturbed at some of his choices. I felt powerless over everything in my life. The psychiatrist wanted to put me out on medical leave for a week. I agreed instead to take off Thursday through Monday for a long Labor Day weekend. Tom was going to Charleston, my favorite place, for a job interview and I went along. While he was busy, I slept most of each day, completely exhausted mentally, physically, and emotionally. But thank God it was not last Labor Day weekend when John was so ill and going into kidney failure.

SINCE JOHN GOT SICK

Allison—Fall, Year Two

John had an "infiltrate." They "blew out" the vein yesterday at dialysis, and he was terrified that the new fistula was ruined. They said it was okay, but they couldn't use that arm for a week, and so they would have to go back to using the chest catheter. The infiltrate was painful, purple and swollen, and John was furious at the doctor's callousness. I drove him to dialysis the next time, going back and forth from work in Easley. I would pick him up today at 3:30 and then take him to the Greenville vascular surgeon.

As I was driving in the right-hand lane, a car coming out of a side street suddenly pulled out in front of me. I saw her eyes, that she saw me, and then she was pulling out anyway, less than ten feet away. As I braked, I knew this was going to be bad, that I was the one going to be in the hospital if I lived. There was impact, windshield glass all over me, air bag imploding against my chest. My horn was stuck, blaring. I knew only to reach into the glass at my feet, pick up my cell phone, and call John before I passed out. "I can't come get you," I said. "I've been in an accident. I'll be going to the emergency room."

John got to the emergency room before I did, having called a friend to get him. My friend Andrea came from Easley and then my friend Libba. I worried about John, his arm, his missed vascular surgery appointment, but he didn't leave me. Miraculously, I wasn't hurt, only bruised and shaken. My car was totaled.

I didn't remember how we got home—John probably got someone to bring him his car. He called Tom in Columbia who wanted to come. John and I collapsed in our respective bedrooms, texting throughout the next day, neither able to get up. Finally I agreed for Tom to come that night. He did, crowded in with us and was wonderful, getting us meals, and on Saturday, taking me to release my car from impound. On Monday, John drove himself to the vascular surgeon, and Tom took me to work and then to get a rental car.

Tom left on Tuesday morning to go to Charleston for his own medical appointment. He had been so wonderful that I allowed myself to believe in him, in our future together, even though our interactions had been limited the past year. He left, and I didn't see him again. He went completely off radar, relapsing into old behaviors, with no one seeing or hearing from him from that Tuesday night until the following Monday morning when he called a friend in Charleston who, in turn, called me. I had been checking with police and hospitals in Charleston since Friday. I didn't want to talk to him, not then or ever. When I had finally decided to completely trust him, he disappeared. I had so much hope for that relationship and again I was disillusioned by my own choosing. I couldn't talk about it. That was the lowest point in the whole journey since John got sick.

John had wanted a dog for years. When he was four, we got a black Lab puppy named Mac who chased a laughing John on his Big Wheel up and down the driveway. They grew up together until Mac died the year of the divorce. Mac was a good dog who knew his place and stayed outside.

John wanted a big dog who stayed in the house. I told him he could do whatever he wanted when he had his own place again.

One day I saw a newspaper picture of a dog advertised by the animal shelter and showed it to John. He took this as my consent for him to get a dog. He continued to look online for days, showing me dogs he liked. Then one Friday he texted me that he was driving to North Carolina to look at a dog. Mostly I was happy that he felt like getting out and said only my usual, "Be careful."

The next text, several hours later, was a picture of a chocolate puppy lying on John's thigh as he drove the truck home. I left work knowing that our household had just increased to three.

John told me that the puppy was a mix of chocolate Lab and Bull Mastiff. What he didn't tell me—his sister did—was that Pippen's mother weighed 120 pounds and his father close to 200.

Pip was maybe the single-most healing thing in his life since he got sick. Initially she slept with him and from the beginning, he got up early to take her out. She gave him a reason to get out of bed and to go for walks, and she was his most consistent companion. She also chewed my deck, dug holes in my back yard, and sent my cat into fulltime exile outside. But she was the sweetest dog ever, with limpid brown eyes and velvety ears.

During this time, I was working on my health. I had stopped taking the prescription anti-inflammatory medication and was taking herbal meds instead. I was trying another anti-depressant. I scheduled a colonoscopy. John took me for the procedure and was my caregiver when I got home; all was well. And in answer to our request on CarePages, several people were considering being donors. We directed them to call the Living Donor Transplant Coordinator at Duke.

I knew that two close friends seriously considered the possibility; at what point they decided to stop or did not meet the requirements, I did not know. Another young man, who had exactly John's birth date, also went through the testing. But it was a stranger, responding to a plea from Vic at his work, who came closest. She got all the way through the testing process only to learn that her kidneys were deemed too small for John. Mid-November, our hopes fell sharply.

I never met this woman, did not even know her name, and could not comprehend her willingness, her altruism. I did not have that in me, to do something so selfless for a stranger.

The odds for successful transplant were greater with living donation. The surgery could be scheduled, the recipient was prepared, and the organ had only to travel to the next operating room. During each of the past five years, more than 6,200 organ transplants came from living donors.

A living donor needed to be in good overall health and free from uncontrolled high blood pressure, diabetes, cancer, HIV/AIDS, hepatitis, and organ disease. Some facilities participated in paired donation or paired exchange programs, in which one incompatible donor pairs with another compatible recipient in a "trade" of donors.

John had been volunteering some at Baptist Easley, thinking he would see if he liked Health Information Management. The HIM staff and the volunteers loved him. One day the volunteer coordinator told me, "He is such a sweet young man. I would give him a kidney if I could, but I am Type B."

Both this woman and the willing altruistic donor impressed me deeply. *I am a good match. I can do this*, I thought. It was the week of Thanksgiving when I called Vic and said, "We need to do this. If I am the donor, can you work it out to be the caregiver, be there with him, *stay* with him for a month after?" He said yes, and I said, "I am calling Duke to tell them I want to proceed."

My next step was to see a urologist. For some reason, there seemed to be a shortage of those specialists in the area. I couldn't get an appointment until mid-December.

Again it was the annual marketing conference, this time in North Carolina. I was grateful for a few days' respite.

In an afternoon free time at the conference, I was blessed with time at the inn's spa. It was a serendipitous experience, another realm for me. After trying the steam and saunas and various hot and cold mineral pools, I sat in the "quiet room" in front of a stone fireplace, holding a cup of steaming plum blossom tea and staring into the fire. I felt drained in every way. I closed my eyes, hearing the fire's small noises, smelling the fragrant tea, feeling the warmth of the cup in my hands, tasting the delicate flavor, praying to feel again some sense of energy and purpose for my life. Random thoughts crossed my mind: of my son, the uncertainty of his future and mine; the hurt and loss of the dream and man I'd loved; the state of the country and world, that nothing was certain anymore. Then, with my eyes open, I took in the winter sky through the window, bare trees, dried eucalyptus on the mantle. After a half-hour, I got up, not feeling much different but aware of time. Realizing I still had some time left, I hesitantly approached the lap pool. Years ago, I used to swim fairly regularly. I hadn't swum in so long and I had felt so old and broken, I was hesitant to try. Did I even remember how? But I took a breath and started a crawl. Almost miraculously, I was moving through the water. My arms and legs did what they were supposed to do and soon I had finished a lap. Then another. Gingerly, I tried a side-stroke, one lap each side. Then a breast stroke, then a backstroke. I stopped and climbed out of the pool, quietly amazed at what had just happened. Did my body know more than my mind? Was it possible to heal past the trauma of this year and continue forging through the rest of my life, however long that may be and with whatever it might hold?

That night at the banquet, the seven strangers at the round table with me talked of trips to Italy, Australia, the Red Sea; of spas in Austria, of scuba and sky diving. I was silent. Who would want to hear about the trauma of my life?

Then one of the winning ads flashed up on the screen. It showed an attractive middle-aged woman—an "altruistic donor"—who had given a kidney to a stranger. "I'm not doing anything special," she stressed, with an almost frustrated expression, as though frequently misunderstood. "It's something I can do. It helps someone else have a chance at a better life."

A second ad, still for that hospital's transplant program, showed the photo of a young athlete whose sudden death benefitted four people; those four strangers told how one of the young man's organs had given each of them life. "I think of that young man every day, and thank him," one recipient says.

Tears in my eyes, I leaned over to the young scuba diver beside me and said, "I am trying to give a kidney to my son." Suddenly I didn't feel quite so old and used up any more.

John—Transplant Testing, Fall Year Two

Although both willing and sharing A+ blood type with me, my dad was unable to donate because of his blood pressure meds and Megan wasn't allowed to because she was still in her childbearing years. A friend or two mentioned the possibility of testing, but when it came down to it, they didn't want to pull the trigger. (Which I absolutely don't blame them for.) Even a nurse I had never met went through the strenuous testing process.

After all my options seemed to slip away, I assumed I would be on dialysis for several years until some poor soul tragically died and his or her family was generous enough to donate the organs, a situation I was trying not to think about. There are different waiting lists depending on the hospital you plan to use. I believe my estimate was between three-to-five years, but I had heard I could be bumped up the list because I was fairly young.

My mom told me she wanted to get tested to see if she could donate, and at the time I kind of brushed it off, I guess. Like all the women in her family she is tiny, and I assumed one of her kidneys wouldn't be able to replace my two kidneys. I was also living with her and she was helping me to live on a daily basis, as well as working full time at the hospital. And finally, she was my mom and I was supposed to protect her, not let her get cut open on an operating table and risk death, health problems, work problems, insurance problems, etc. But she worked hard to get off medication for arthritis and jumped through every hoop they threw at her until she was finally accepted to donate one of her kidneys to me.

Being a mother-to-child transplant was a much better match than just about anybody, except identical twins. Some receiving twins are able to live their lives without the horrid anti- rejection meds because their bodies can't tell the difference! I'm confident Mom would've done anything to see me get off of dialysis. She was the only one who saw me come home with shirts covered in blood from problems sticking my fistula with the huge needles at dialysis. Or the times the insertion of the two thick gauge needles would "infiltrate," or basically go all the way through the fistula, causing my upper arm to bruise and hurt much worse the next time I'd get stuck. Some days were okay, but many were hell and left me wondering how much longer I wanted to live in that much pain and constant fatigue. At times I wondered what exactly was worth living for, what qualities I needed to have in my future, and which things I could live without.

Allison—Winter, Year Two

December 14 was the awaited urology appointment. The cystoscope was not pleasant but everything was fine. The doctor sent his report to Duke and gave me the films to take with me. My internist had also sent her records of my recent physical. John had a second procedure and an angiogram at the dialysis center to address more problems with his blood flow and access. It didn't seem to help, and he had another painful infiltrate a few days later. I came in to see him standing in the kitchen, crying in pain and frustration.

I had done all I could and was waiting on Duke. My appointment was scheduled for January 23.

Christmas Eve, John went to his father's and I went to the Gowers alone. The next day I drove to my cousin Elaine's in Atlanta. Everyone was supportive and hopeful for my ability to give John a kidney.

At the beginning of January, we learned that John would no longer have the COBRA insurance coverage that we had continued to pay for. The small business where he worked could no longer afford to offer its employees an insurance product. I tried to get a Medicare supplement for John but learned that the state of South Carolina did not offer a supplement to anyone under the age of 65. My inquiries made it all the way to the SC Department of Insurance. The answer to my question, "How can this be?!" was "We just don't." Ah, South Carolina. Desperately—John would not be able to get the transplant without co-insurance—I kept working with Blue Cross Blue Shield, with whom he'd had uninterrupted coverage, and finally got him a supplement with them through the state of North Carolina. It would cost $650 per month but would cover meds that could cost thousands per month.

Finally it was January 23. My friend Catherine drove me up and stayed with me all day; I was so grateful not to be alone. It felt weird to be at Duke without John. It made me sad that I was healthy and he was not. I was also aware that something inside me—a power, a force—was pushing me forward, greater than my fears and worries. I prayed every day for John, for the fullness of his life: health, work, home, partner, children, meaning. I held him in that Light.

Jeremiah 29:11 stayed with me: "'For I know the plans I have for you,' declares the Lord, 'plans to prosper you and not harm you, plans to give you hope and a future.'" I held on to this verse for both John and me.

I again talked to the donor advocate. I told her of my concerns regarding money. John's Medicare would pay for the surgery, but there were follow-up doctors' appointments, hotel expenses for the ten days in Durham, travel costs for my daughter and cousins, time away from work. She told me about a grant that I could apply for through the National Kidney Foundation. Subsequent appointments with a social worker and psychologist went well. They all were more concerned with John having a caregiver in place. I would come back with John and Vic and Janet in February for more tests for me and another evaluation for John.

National Heart Day fell on February 3. I wore a scarf patterned with pink and red hearts with my blue jeans and white shirt. It felt appropriate for this day at Duke for us. John and I got blood drawn first. They took thirteen vials from him and nine from me. We each had appointments, so I was back and forth with him and Vic and Janet as much as I could be. Often I was the one who knew the details of his illness history; much of it he was not aware of or didn't remember. John texted me as I was finishing in X-ray, and I hurried in to his exam room. The doctor greeted me sternly and said, "So, you are the kidney."

"I hope so," I responded.

As John finished his day with Vic and Janet, I almost ran back to radiology for a CT scan of my kidneys. This was the step that had excluded the other prospective donor. As the contrast went into my arm, I prayed that I would be suitable.

As soon as I was done, John texted me that he was in the front drive, itching to get on the road, *to go*, intense as he always was about leaving Duke. I was feeling weak and slightly nauseated and wanted to stop for something to eat. I gave up, lay back in the seat, and felt a little sorry for myself. The nephrologist had given his approval for a Living Donor donation, and Vic and Janet had signed the agreement for the necessary caregiver responsibilities. Now we waited to hear about me.

The transplant coordinator called me on February 8. My labs were back. Everything looked good except for one number. My GFR (which has to do with kidney function) was 81.9; good is 90-120, acceptable is 80. She stated that the number was fine for me, but the transplant committee would have to decide if that was good enough for John at his young age.

I thought, *wouldn't anything be better than the anguish of dialysis?* But it was out of my hands. Even though it was my body and my willingness, the final decision was not mine. I showed the medical director at my hospital my lab numbers and asked him what he thought. He circled one and handed it back to me. "There's only one number on there that concerns me. 58."

He was, of course, referring to my age, which I could do nothing about.

Megan, working with my second cousin, Wendy, had started a social media fundraising campaign. And my friend Ellen was organizing a local campaign as well.

On February 9, I prayed in the hospital chapel, part of my daily routine. I didn't want John to be disappointed again. I knew that all I could do was be with him, no matter what. I thought that is what God promises to each of us. I bought a mug in the hospital gift shop. It had a pink heart on it, reminding me of the scarf that I had worn at Duke, with the word, Believe.

That afternoon, the transplant coordinator called again. They were accepting me as a donor for John! I was so happy, so grateful, that I could not even cry. John didn't answer his phone but Megan did, and Vic. Vic told me that he wished it could be he, that many people would be praying for me and he would be one. I told a few people at work and soon there was a bud vase on my desk with two pink roses and then a balloon that said, "An angel is watching over you." I was so grateful for the kindness of the people I worked with.

I finally reached John who hadn't been able to wake up. I told him the news as he struggled to get to dialysis.

That night John asked me how to get into the local newspaper something he had written. Surfing the Internet at dialysis that day, he'd realized that Valentine's was also National Donor Day. He'd written a piece for it that I knew should be an op-ed. I told him I would check with the paper's editorial page editor who was a friend. She responded positively and I sent it to her. The health reporter also picked up on our news and wanted to do a story. Over the next days, John and I were featured with a photo on the front page of the newspaper, his op-ed ran on Sunday, and we were also on the local TV station. The story was online and was picked up by USA Today online. I was so proud for what he wrote:

> While most people celebrate Valentine's Day today, my family and I will be celebrating National Donor Day and my mother's ability and willingness to donate one of her kidneys to me.
> In April of 2010, I was diagnosed with a rare autoimmune disease called Wegener's Granulomatosis. After the diagnosis at Baptist Easley Hospital, I spent most of the following eight months hospitalized at Greenville Hospital System and Duke University Medical

Center. For nine weeks that summer I was in an induced coma, surviving only with the constant support of multiple machines and medications. Then I began my recovery at Roger C. Peace Rehabilitation Center. With the help of doctors, nurses, friends and family I worked through the physical and mental process of being back with the living. Emotions were intense, sometimes senses were intense (I could smell people coming before I could even hear them), and I was physically exhausted as therapists pushed me to begin walking, dressing, and generally taking care of myself again. By December 2010, the disease was pronounced to be in remission.

Unfortunately, the disease itself, and some of the toxic drugs used to combat it, led to End Stage Renal Disease, meaning that I would need four hours of dialysis three days a week to do the job my kidneys no longer could. This also meant never leaving Greenville for more than a day without weeks of preparation, paperwork, and updating shots. Some of the toughest people I've ever known I met through dialysis—like people without legs and the many who come by ambulance and never complain. But it is not a fun place to be. And the only way I can ever leave is for someone to give me a kidney. That's not something you can just go around asking for.

After several attempts by my family, friends and a couple of strangers failed to find a matching kidney, my hopes were low. Thankfully, my mother has kept herself healthy and wouldn't take "no" for an answer. After being turned down once, she tried everything the transplant team suggested and went through the testing process again. We found out last week that she will be able to donate, therefore giving me life again! There are many possible complications, including dangerous clotting issues and the possibility of my body rejecting the foreign kidney. But for now we are positive and I am thankful.

Not many people know (I didn't until recently) that Valentine's Day is also National Donor Day. Unfortunately, we live in a world where everyone will meet someone during his or her life that needs some kind of blood, tissue or organ donation. Donation not only leads to individuals getting off dialysis but can give eyesight to people, help burn victims, save limbs and, ultimately, save lives. There are an estimated 600,000 people waiting on life-saving transplants and donations. If you've ever thought of helping people around you or leaving a legacy, remember that for each person that donates tissue and organs, 50 people can benefit.

Start by giving blood, which is, pound for pound, the least trouble and the most effective donation option. It gave me peace of mind to pretend the blood I received was actually from friends and not strangers. If you know someone in the hospital who is receiving blood transfusions, you can give in their name (regardless of blood type) and it will be taken off their bill. I ended up having around 35 transfusions, and most were covered by a blood drive put on by my friends. See how you feel after giving blood in your community, and then consider joining the South Carolina Donor Registry. This can be done through your local DMV, or several websites, including: www. lifepoint-sc.org and www.donatelifesc.org.

There isn't anything I can say to show how thankful I am for the family, friends, doctors, nurses and community that have helped during the longest two years of my life. At least I can try to show my gratitude by encouraging people to help others this Valentine's Day.

If you'd like to know more about my story, feel free to join www. carepages.com (free) and search for jggreene. My family and I have been posting updates here from the beginning of my sickness.

A fundraiser was scheduled for early March at the home of a friend. Donations were coming in to the online website. My Family Medical Leave of Absence (FMLA) had been approved. I was notified that the national grant I had applied for would pay for all my additional expenses. Then we learned that the surgery would be April 9, the Monday following Easter. John would be admitted on Good Friday. That seemed appropriate. I was aware that it would be almost two years to the date, April 13, 2010, that he was first hospitalized.

Megan in Tennessee and my cousin Diane in Florida bought their plane tickets. Megan would come up for the surgeries, staying Saturday until Wednesday. Her mother-in-law would help keep Millie who was not yet one. Diane, along with her sister Elaine, would arrive on Tuesday and stay with me the additional week at Duke, drive me back to Greenville, and stay with me there as long as I needed them. Two co-workers from my hospital drove up for the day of surgery, and co-workers from my home marketing department donated paid time off (PTO) hours for me so that I would not lose income. Everything was working out, moving forward, being taken care of.

Soon John found a house nearby that he could afford to rent with a roommate. He and his friend moved in a couple of weeks before the surgery. He was eager to be on his own again. A co-worker of mine installed an electric fence for him so that Pip could be outside some. And knowing our need for someone to keep Pip, my friend Catherine reached out to her veterinarian daughter-in-law who graciously offered for Pip to stay with her family for the six weeks that John would be in Durham.

In late February, I learned that my friend Gayle Price had been given two weeks to live; hospice had been called in. Only a few months ago was she diagnosed with cancer. I had seen her just before Christmas, and she looked wonderful and was in remission. Then suddenly the cancer had returned aggressively. I saw her again just a few days before her death. I could hardly comprehend it. Gayle had been so strong for me, visiting John during Greenville hospital stays, supporting me. She was always so fierce. How could she be gone? And John lived on.

John and I went to Gayle's funeral on March 9. It was incredibly sad and still unbelievable to me. People there wished us well on the upcoming transplant. I could almost see Gayle's bright face beaming up at John, telling him she was proud of him and that all would be well.

About three weeks before the surgery, I began seeing a flashing light in my right eye. Fearing a detached retina, I quickly got an appointment with an ophthalmologist, who happened to be the one my mother saw decades ago. He could not find anything wrong with my eye, but he prayed with me for both surgeries and told me, "Your mother would be so proud."

The rest of the month was a whirlwind of preparing to be away from work for a month, writing thank-you notes to all the contributors, and getting things in order at home. Every day I talked to my body, telling one kidney—I wouldn't know which until the surgeon looked inside and decided—that it was going to go live in John's body and help him. I prayed for a successful transplant. Then it was Thursday, April 5, and John and I were once again driving to Duke for yet another night at the Millennium Hotel.

John's admission on Friday went smoothly. He was used to the ritual of Argatroban drip, dialysis. I would not be admitted until early Monday morning; I would only be hospitalized a couple of days. Saturday morning I slept in a bit, alone in the hotel room. Small thoughts that morning—scanning the health of my body, wondering about potential damage to my health, always the sadness of what had happened to John, that it was Holy Saturday and quiet in the tomb with sorrow about, knowing that many people were praying for us. I got up to get juice and a bagel and dressed to go see John at the hospital. My biggest task today was to pick up Megan at the Durham airport.

Megan landed, bringing Easter baskets and bunny ears. When we were back at John's room, I released my load of responsibility, carried for more than two years. She and John went for a walk-about. I crawled into John's hospital bed. The push even the last few weeks had further taxed my diminished energy. *I just want to sleep,* I thought.

Later that afternoon, I went back to the ICU where we spent so many weeks. No one else wanted to go; I managed it alone. It was something I had to do. I pushed the intercom button and asked for Lauren or Vickie.

Vickie came out. She recognized me and hugged me, telling me that Lauren had moved to another town. She was happy about the transplant. I was almost overwhelmed, remembering those hopeless days in the summer of 2010. I shuddered when I saw the conference room. That experience was still too close; my mind could not comprehend the terror I experienced there.

Early Monday morning, Megan and I left the hotel, arriving at Duke at 5:30 a.m. She had the unique position of having her mother and her only sibling in side-by-side operating rooms. They would start with me, and when the surgeon thought everything was okay, they would put John under. The whole procedure would take four to six hours. By 7 a.m., John and I were both in pre-op and I had been given a small amount of sedation. Immediately I could feel it take effect. "I'm going . . . ," I said, and tried to wave to John in his pre-op room as I was wheeled by. Then I was gone.

It has been somewhat of a joke in our family that one aspirin can put me out, while John needed enough medication to choke a horse.

In Recovery I woke momentarily and heard Megan say, "John is fine, and the kidney worked immediately!" Later she told me that at one point the nurse asked me if I wanted something to drink, and I said clearly, "Unsweet tea, please." I didn't remember saying that, or the tea. I remembered waking up later that night in pain and turning back into it, into the sleep again, to escape it, and the next afternoon, a nurse telling me I could leave that day if I wanted to. My answer was to fall back into sleep and not wake again until the following morning.

During those 48-or-so hours, John was in intensive care, having a rough time. His surgery was much more extensive than mine. He was cut all the way down his middle, about a foot, and there were other complications, too. Again, as in times before, he was in excruciating, unrelieved pain. But I was unaware.

Megan left on Wednesday to go back to her baby and husband, and my two cousins took over. I was so comfortable with them; my earliest memories were of being with them, my closest older cousins whom I always wanted to be with and catch up to. Back to the Millennium Hotel we went – home to me on so many trips—where I slept for a week. I tried to eat and move about and then would go back to sleep. I was so glad they were there for me when I had no other family.

On Friday, they took me back to the hospital to see John, now in a regular room. At this point, he looked and felt better than I did. He said he felt better a couple of days after the surgery than he had in the past two years. That the kidney worked immediately was yet another boon; according to the nephrologists, many patients had to stay on dialysis for several days while the new kidney decided to work.

After my one-week post-op check, Elaine and Diane drove me to Greenville and stayed several more days. I told them to leave; I was fine by myself. I just wanted to sleep.

John—Transplant Surgery, April, Year Three

For the countless reasons the two of us are alike, when it comes to anesthesia my mom and I are total opposites. For me to actually have a noticeable decrease in my pain or consciousness, they usually give me way more meds than they're comfortable with. At one point I told an anesthesiologist that I was still in serious pain, and he told me if he gave me any more pain meds he was pretty sure my heart would stop.

Mom on the other hand, gets dizzy when they mention Versed and passes out after taking a Tylenol. So as I'm freaking out about my mom and trying to tell them it's going to take a lot more medicine to calm me down and bottles more to knock me out, I see them slowly push my mom by in her bed. She obviously wasn't having the same problems with the meds, so she barely lifted her head up and gave a little wave. I said I loved her and as soon as she was out of sight started crying. As I had said multiple times before, I was rarely scared when I was the patient, but seeing my mom like that made all of the worst possibilities go through my head, and I wondered if I would ever see her again.

The operating surgeon came by one last time to draw where the incision would be made and initial it. That's a practice I always found strange. I'm sure there's a good reason, like you probably wouldn't operate on the wrong person if you saw another doctor's initials on your patient, but I just felt like they were claiming their meat or something. I met the actual operating surgeon only a couple times before and after the transplant. That is understandable. Those men and women are some of the best of the best and literally spend all day with multiple lives relying on their skill. Truthfully, his demeanor gave me confidence from the first time I met him. He didn't talk too much or too loud, although when he spoke it was clear enough for myself and family to understand without patronizing us. He presented himself as fully capable of performing a perfect transplant without treating it as a nonchalant surgery he'd done hundreds of time before.

After he gave the go ahead, I was given more drugs and taken back shortly after. The next thing I remember was waking up to indescribable pain in my stomach. My first thought was that they had somehow moved organs around into the wrong places! There was no way I was supposed to be in that much pain. There isn't really anything you can do for pain of that magnitude. At the beginning, at least, you just have to scream, grit your teeth, and know that it's not going to last forever. Soon the medicine will kick in, but it only helps so much and no body position gives any resemblance of relief. My dad was in recovery with me, and Megan was there for my Mom. When Megan came to my room, I immediately asked how mom was doing, and she chuckled and said the first thing Mom asked was how was I doing.

They wanted to make sure the kidney was working, so I was on enough IV fluids that they were coming in one tube and going out of another at about the same rate for at least 24 hours, but overall I was told everything was a success. I think Mom was in more pain than she expected, but she came to my room a few days after surgery. We have a picture of the two of us lying on my bed, and was the first time in over two years that my face and skin had natural color as opposed to the ghostly white/grey color. We both had big smiles.

She was able to leave within a few days, and I wasn't far behind her, walking out on two feet with my leather weekend bag over my shoulder and hope in my heart. I was even entertaining the idea that I could participate in the Kidney Walk coming up in a few weeks. She went back home to Greenville where her cousins (basically sisters) took care of her for a while. Because there was still a possibility that my body would see the new kidney as foreign and attack/reject it, I was able to leave Duke but told to stay in Durham for a couple more weeks so I could come in for check-ups and be close if anything serious happened. My dad and Janet stayed with me at a nice little apartment they had rented close to campus. It was perfect, really. Quiet, first floor, close to the parking lot, and close to the hospital.

The transplant brought with it a whole new regimen of medication including some pretty strong anti-rejection drugs. I think the summation of meds and recent events knocked me out for at least a couple of days once I got to the apartment. I slept on the couch a lot of the time only to be wakened by my dad or Janet handing me whatever concoction of meds I was supposed to take that hour as well as forcing me to eat or drink. There were still times in those early days that I had no clue if things were working right and feared that I had made my mom go through that much pain for the whole thing to be unsuccessful.

My dad was down to the final days of work he could miss so, thankfully, Janet stuck it out with me the last week or so. I slowly started getting off the couch and trying to walk around. The dumpster for the apartment complex was past the pool and tennis courts, so it was my first goal. It was a couple hundred yards at the most, but being able to make that confidently felt better than any winning field goal I kicked, any race I won, any soccer game that I sacrificed my life for, and even better than pinning a senior to the mat as a freshman at my first wrestling match.

It wasn't just that I was walking that distance, but also that I was allowing my mind to think about my future again. It had been a while since I had done that, at least in a positive sense. After it ended with Anne, I wasn't sure what life would entail. At least she understood what had happened to me, why I hadn't been around, why I gained weight and had stretch marks and lived with my mom for a little while. Even some of my closest friends didn't understand all the things going on with me (including Wegener's), and people I had never met wouldn't know whether I was even safe to be near. (I'm not contagious, by the way.)

Now I was able to look beyond that. I started thinking about an old girlfriend I hadn't talked to in years, but had never gotten over. Maybe even that was possible again! I also couldn't wait to get back to work, get back in shape and lose some of the weight gained from daily Prednisone doses of 1,000 milligrams. There isn't much I can do for the stretch marks or the bulging fistula in my right bicep that took 40 staples to close. There's also not much I can do to hide the scar from the kidney transplant incision where surgeons cut through my abs and gently inserted my mother's kidney. That also took 40+ staples on the outside (and countless stitches

TRANSPLANT

inside) to close and is now a 14-inch scar running down the middle of my abdomen.

And I don't blame anyone for looking. I just wish they knew that it took the strength of an entire family, group of amazing friends, and doctors and nurses who spend their entire lives studying to keep people like me alive and able to live a quasi-normal life. As cliché as it may sound, my scars help me remember everything I went through, down to the recovery room where I was taken after the six-plus hour fistula surgery, and when I became comfortable enough to remove my stitches and staples by myself. There's a small percentage of people on the planet who can look at my scars and know what kind of pain they came with.

5

Darkness

Allison—Spring, Year Three

I WASN'T PREPARED FOR how bad I would feel after the surgery. The doctors minimized that part. Initially I planned to be out of work three to four weeks, but I stayed out the full four and then worked only part-time for weeks five and six.

I don't know how much of it was emotional, my fatigue. So much, so many terrible things had happened continuously the past two years. Besides all of John's sickness, six months earlier I'd had an accident, totaled my car, and finally ended a serious multi-year relationship. And I hadn't had the time or opportunity to deal with any of that while watching John try to survive dialysis and attempting to get myself approved as a donor. Now my body was missing a major organ.

For the first time in two years, I had time to feel. Not pushing to get to work or take care of John, my only task was to heal physically. I didn't want to get out of bed. Darkness different from shock, trauma and fear settled in and stayed.

Some tears finally needled the backs of my eyes and one or two edged out. For John and all that he'd suffered. For everything I had endured. Such sadness. Such loss.

It took it out of me. Those words were in my head on waking one morning, two-plus weeks after the surgery. "It," meaning the kidney donation but also so much more. I had no energy for anything those weeks.

This earthquake that happened when John got sick: how could I go on in life not knowing when something like that would happen again? Despite God's presence and miracles and blessings, I didn't want my earth to move again and all that I knew to be true to shift continuously beneath me. I couldn't face it. So I hid in my bed.

I had always been a runner of sorts, emotionally if not so much physically. Whenever the anxiety, quick energy, got too intense, I would run or at least walk at length meditatively. Ever since John got sick, my knees hurt too bad to even walk much.

I tried to walk a little at the mall and then finally at the gym where I'd gone religiously for years. I crept around the indoor track like an eighty-year-old. Regulars there were glad to see me, asked me how I was doing. I appreciated it, but it didn't really help. I was alone in my sense of no one understanding, no one knowing what it was like, of what I'd been through.

I remembered months earlier, when John was at Duke and I stayed in Greenville to work, people would smile and ask conversationally, "How are you?" and I would think, *How do I answer that? My son is dying and I am not with him.* I couldn't possibly say how I really was, or I would not be functional. I would never get anything done on my job or keep body and soul together. So I just kept it all inside and went through the motions.

Now the motions were even more limited. This time was full of reverberating psychic pain, echoing deeper and deeper.

I stopped by a local lunch spot. The owner came around the counter, hugged me, wouldn't let me pay. Tears came to my eyes. Maybe it's the little graces, the small acts of kindness, that hold us. Even when the earth splits and our innards fall out.

During this time, John was experiencing ups and downs in Durham. His creatinine had been high and two-plus weeks after surgery, doctors at Duke wanted to re-hospitalize him and do a kidney biopsy. John flatly refused and came back to Greenville. His father would take him back for weekly checks for the next few weeks. He was glad to get back home and see Pip. At the next check-up, he learned he had a bladder infection that only immuno-suppressed people get; the transplant team cut back his Cellcept dosage. In following weeks, he continued to have various infections and fatigue.

I had dreams, mostly about John when he was younger, that he was hurt, almost dying. I realized how close to John's near-death episodes I still was, the trauma of that experience still with me. At some level, I was afraid all the time of his dying. I continued to pray for healing, his and mine.

Allison—Summer, Year Three

John had pinned so many hopes on the transplant, that he would have his life back, and two months after, that had not happened. Even though he had moved out and now lived with a roommate in a small rental house nearby, many days he did not feel well at all. I went with him back to Duke for his rheumatology appointment. We stopped to eat on the way. He was silent across from me in the booth. I noticed the pallor of his skin and the trembling of his fingers, the scar at his throat and down his arm. I wanted to reach across the table and take him in my arms, all six-foot-one of him. Instead I commented on the song that was playing—the Indigo girls doing a Joan Baez original, I thought. He didn't know either. We agreed that his dad or Megan would know.

Drs. Allen and George were wonderful as usual, full of encouragement. Dr. George exclaimed, "It's only been two years since you almost died! You look great!" New residents came in to see the "miracle boy," the term that followed him, at least at Duke Rheumatology. Here, they understood who he was, what he'd been through.

I had researched holistic healing and learned about Duke Integrative Medicine. I asked Dr. Allen about it, and she was not opposed. Before we left Duke, we stopped by the Center and picked up a brochure. Besides medical evaluation, they offered nutritional counseling, acupuncture, yoga, and various other therapies. I made John appointments to coincide with a return Duke visit in September.

Before leaving Durham we stopped at Loco Pops. Megan and Anne had found the homemade popsicle store last summer, bringing dripping pops to John before he went to ICU.

Some days for John were good days. I could tell when he texted me early on a Saturday morning to say he was going to the jockey lot and did I want any plums? Then there were the other days when he didn't reply to my texts until mid-afternoon and I knew that he hadn't been able to get up.

A singularly important person in both John's and my journey the past year in Greenville was Dr. Joanne Skaggs. We had first met her as chief resident when John was initially transferred to Greenville's ICU. Now in private practice, she managed his care on an almost-weekly basis and tried to keep me sane. I don't know which was the harder task. I had texted her at odd hours, evenings and weekends, and she responded quickly. She had kept John out of the hospital on several occasions. When I started my transplant journey, she became my doctor, too. I have cried with her, and she has prayed with me. God definitely placed her, and her assistant Paula, in our lives.

Two months after the surgery, I developed a strange condition on the top of my left foot. At work, my ankle felt stiff and then I noticed that it was red and swollen. Soon there was pain and I was having difficulty walking. This condition occurred two more times over the next months. Nothing specific showed up on X-rays or in labs. Prednisone and antibiotics helped. My unspoken pre-transplant fears returned: that something would be wrong, I wouldn't be able to work, that there would be no one to help me, physically, financially, or emotionally. Loneliness seeped in to erode me.

The lab work showed that my sodium was dangerously low, likely contributing to my tiredness. My doctor thought it was s a side effect of the antidepressant I had been taking and wanted me to stop it. *Really?* I had some concern but was willing to try.

I started doing hot yoga as therapy for the arthritis in my knees. I loved it; it was also mental therapy. For an hour-and-a-half in the 105-degree room, all I had to think about was trying to breathe and not pass out. What a relief. The exhaustion after was a good feeling.

But I continued to be exhausted all the time. Every weekday morning, I dragged myself out of bed to get to work. On weekends I slept. I hesitated to commit to doing anything in the evenings for fear I would get too tired. It was a terrible feeling and one I imagine that John knew only too well. I was still struggling with arthritis in my knees, plus the random bouts of inflammation with my foot.

In August, we went to Sewanee for a brief visit. After the five-hour trip, we walked with Megan, and Millie in her stroller, to a nearby park. John was exhausted before we got back. I was also tired and rested on Megan's bed. I told her, "John is not OK, and neither am I." She agreed but didn't know what to do about it. It seemed like the others had gone on with their lives, and John and I were left behind.

John—On Crying and Dying, Spring/Summer, Year Three

Regardless of the circumstance—pain, fear, regret—I have never been comfortable crying. Not by myself and especially not in front of others. Though still true today, I am less ashamed after all the practice I've had.

My biggest obstacles for moving forward are fear and uncertainty. Most Wegener's patients relapse, I will likely need more kidney transplants (depending on how long I live), my meds are likely to cause bladder cancer and severe bone decay, and I get normal illnesses much more easily because I am immunosuppressed.

If a doctor could tell me that my future would be long and hard, I would be okay with that. I am stronger physically than mentally.

The worst part about dying would be leaving my family behind. My mom was an only child and she hated it, so she wanted two kids of her own. She told Megan and me that she had both of us so we would always be there for each other.

Megan reminded me of that while she was studying in Italy and I was having trouble staying sober and out of jail in high school. When I heard her say that, I immediately wondered how I had forgotten hearing it so many times when we were little, and I started to cry. It was a Friday during my senior year of high school, and I was planning on going to USC that afternoon for a semi-formal with my friend's girlfriend's twin sister. Instead my parents gave me an ultimatum to leave immediately for rehab, or I would be kicked out of both of their houses, my car would be sold, and I would be cut off. I was fine with all of those things and ready to take on the challenge out of spite until they played the tape Megan made in Italy and mailed back home. That day I learned how much my sister loved me. That experience also caused me to develop trust issues I may never overcome.

Allison—Fall, Year Three

In September we visited the Duke Integrative Medicine Center. As we walked into the building, I noticed the raised metal script on the stone wall: *Experience the Soul of Duke Medicine.* The words resonated deep within me. I knew this was where we needed to be. I had long been interested in holistic healing, even working part-time for several years at Creative Health in Greenville. I think I had always believed in the interconnectedness of body/mind/spirit. I believed John would find healing here.

He was impressed with the beauty of the facility and went in for an hour-and-a-half, one-on-one yoga session. I walked in the meditative gardens, which included a labyrinth. Seeing a group in progress, I also inquired and learned about the Health Coach certificate program going on there.

I met John after his yoga session, and he said, "Well, I know I can't talk about *it.*" I didn't know what the teacher asked him—maybe just about the scars on his body or his limitations—but he had begun shaking and sweating profusely. Of course I thought that talking about *it* was exactly what he needed to do, that again this was a PTSD reaction, but I knew that he could not be pushed. Next he went for acupuncture, and I got a massage.

Face down on the massage table, I was suddenly crying. When it was time to turn over, with tears still streaming, I told the therapist, "It's not you. I don't know what it is; I hardly ever cry." She only nodded and said, "Tears are healing."

I waited on John in the solarium, which was perfectly still but for the fountain in the center. The acupuncturist came out to talk to me while the treatment was still ongoing with John. She told me that his fatigue was not uncommon. "We see it a lot after trauma, particularly with young people coming back from Afghanistan. Their spirits don't know where they are, or even where they want to be. His is not yet fully back in his body."

This made perfect sense to me. How could his spirit comprehend all the trauma that had gone on with his body? I remembered wondering when John came out of the weeks-long coma, what had he seen, learned, experienced? But he had waked up, like Rip Van Winkle, thinking his twenty-six-year-old life was just as he'd left it and with no particular sense that he had been saved for any special purpose.

On the questionnaire prior to the visit, John had answered that when he remembered feeling happy, he was playing soccer. She told me she had encouraged him to watch videos of soccer to re-engage his muscle memory.

John came out, positive about the acupuncture. We went for some lunch at nearby Nosh. Through the many visits and stays in Durham, the owner knew and remembered John. She was always glad to see him.

The final appointment of the day was with an internal medicine doctor. He spent an hour examining John and then called me back, too. He wanted John to see a nutritionist and a health psychologist there, as well as have follow-up appointments with him, and do acupuncture and yoga as John chose. Because of all the medications he was on, John would never take the herbal supplements that I swore by. The doctor explained that the Center had a million-dollar software program that analyzed contraindications of any supplement with the prescription medications that John was on. He also recommended a counselor there that I should see, someone who had gone through an experience similar to mine. Since John still had co-insurance and also money in the fund, he could afford to do these things. I was practically elated. We scheduled appointments for October.

The doctor reminded us that this was a marathon and not a sprint. He encouraged John to try for a five percent increase in exertion—not a fifty or hundred percent. John had never been one for moderation. I wished he had a health coach, like the all the other sports coaches he'd had in his life.

I was interested in the Health Coaching program myself, even though I knew I couldn't do it for John. I pursued the application process and was accepted into the program, but realized that I didn't have the money. It was almost $10,000, plus days spent at Duke and travel costs. I couldn't afford any more time off, even if I had the money for tuition.

On October 2, John and I went to dinner for his twenty-ninth birthday. The upcoming visits to Duke were the following week. I was looking forward to them and mentioned them to John. He told me that he was not going, that he didn't want to do them. I was so disappointed, I hardly spoke. I knew that I could not force him, that it would do no good. So I would cancel my appointment, too, not wanting to take the time from work or spend the money for the trip on a one-hour counseling session for me. It was a short evening and I went home saddened.

My challenge those days was to pull back my energy from him. I had fought so long and so hard for his life. I had been literally his voice, advocating for his care, for all the weeks he was on the ventilator. I had felt every needle stick, every insult to his body, because I didn't want him to bear it alone. Now I had to let him figure it out.

Near the end of October on a Sunday, I went to visit my friend and Tom's mother, Elizabeth. We had kept in contact and John had gone with me to visit her after the transplant. Her home, with its pine-paneled den was so much like the one I grew up in. It was a comfort to me, as was her loving presence. Out at lunch that day, I learned that Tom was back living with her. I had a physical shock, an immediate fight/flight reaction. I took her home, not going in, and drove back to Greenville. It was none of my business and yet it felt so wrong, as though she had abandoned me. I thought that I could not be in her life anymore.

Another bout of severe depression followed. It was as if in losing Elizabeth, I had lost my last lifeline. I was too exhausted to get out of bed.

I went to see Dr. Skaggs who determined that my thyroid function was low. She started me on two medications, and I stayed out of work for a week. I reminded her that I had stopped taking the antidepressant several months before. She thought I could do without it and wanted me to wait and see how I felt after time on the thyroid medications. I scheduled an appointment with a therapist in Greenville and got in quickly on a cancellation.

At the first session, the counselor began working with me on my post-trauma syndrome, using a technique (EMDR) pioneered by the military. She was also adamant that I get back on an antidepressant. I saw the psychiatrist who sent me for labs. I noticed that the referral paper said, Major Depressive Episode. Great, now I really was mentally ill. (Months later I learned that severe depression often follows kidney donation, a detail I had never heard.)

I saw the counselor almost weekly for a few months, until I couldn't afford it any longer. She didn't take insurance and the sessions were just too expensive. Nothing dramatic occurred, mostly cognitive awareness, but I was better. I also had to stop the hot yoga. It was too dehydrating for me. I didn't know if it had to do with having only one kidney or not, but I couldn't seem to recover/rehydrate enough to stay on top of fatigue.

I joined a weekly small-group women's book study. In it I began to trust some and to see how fear was eating me up. Being aware was not enough to change it. I feared many things but mostly about John, my aloneness, my health and energy, of not enough money, my aging. I prayed for hope and an assurance of a brighter day.

My counselor said that I have "survived by embracing what is. Pain, terror, rage, hopelessness, powerlessness. By embracing and processing (feelings), we act them in or act them out—that's how the psyche heals." I tried to believe that.

I realized that there are many things in my life that hurt, that aren't fair or "right," and it was not all my fault. I began to understand that my post-traumatic stress was not uncontrollable flashbacks but rather energy still tied to that time and place.

John had labs drawn regularly in Greenville for Duke. Again his creatinine was higher than the doctors liked; again they wanted to a do a biopsy, and again he refused. Then a few weeks later, his creatinine was lower than it had been since the transplant. With those labs and monthly visits to the Coumaden clinic, where his blood numbers were frequently up and down, he rode the waves of uncertainty concerning his health.

On one trip to Duke, when he went alone, he came back with a tattoo. All I could think about was the danger, with him on blood thinner medication and being immunosuppressed. But the brand on his forearm was like his mission statement. Looking as though they were typewritten were the words: I STRUGGLE AND ARISE.

It was almost Thanksgiving and Megan and her family were meeting John and me at my cousin's in Atlanta. John brought me beautiful roses, dusky pink, with a card that said, "Thank you for the kidney."

Allison—Winter, Year Three

John was supposed to go to Duke right after Christmas but he was suddenly too sick—a violent reoccurrence of the C. diff, the horrible intestinal bacteria that had hospitalized him before. He was terribly sick for more than a week. He started on one antibiotic, and then Dr. Skaggs called in another. I was waiting at CVS at 9:30 p.m., exhausted from worry and work, when out of the blue, I began getting texts from Tom, berating me for what a "piece of work" I was, that I let other people sway me, that he'd planned to give me his grandmother's diamond ring. . . . I tried to ignore the texts, but the sudden attack felt so wrong, hurt so deeply. I was weeping in the pharmacy line at the unfairness of all this and knowing that John needed to be in the hospital. Finally the prescription was ready and I took it to him, along with more Gatorade.

John made it through the C. diff without hospitalization, only by sheer force of will, I knew. I was grateful to him; his hospitalizations were too hard. His Duke visit had to be postponed. But I took him up mid-January and he got a good report, not having to return for eight weeks.

Anytime driving on I-85 North around our town, I flash back to drives to Duke. Mostly these are comforting flashbacks. Today with John, for a check-up at the Duke clinic, I think again, *There is no place in the world like Duke University Medical Center.* I remember driving in the first time, or the many times after, seeing the clump of buildings appearing past the curve just after the highway exit ramp. Then seeing people scurrying around, walking from building to building, navigating crosswalks. People of every type—different nationalities; variously dressed, some in professional white coats, others in T-shirts or scrubs; many in wheelchairs; children and seniors. Every time I approached Duke, an emotion rose in my throat. I think it is love—or at least gratitude, hope, a feeling of safety, and even of reverence.

On my first trip to Duke as the hotel shuttle waited at the red light to turn into the circular drive, I looked at the medical center outlined in neon and knew that we would likely return to this place throughout the years. Just as its tall cathedral spire is visible from all parts of the campus, Duke is a touchstone, a place to recalibrate, to mark an event that changed our lives irrevocably.

Allison—Spring, Year Four

It was April, a year after the transplant. I decided to put sod in my front yard. A man offered to help and he, along with John and the man who cut my grass, took on the endeavor. It was a feat for all of us, but finally the sod was laid and I had to put only the direct cost of it on my credit card. I watered it diligently and was encouraged by bright green growth whenever I looked out my window.

My left foot was hurting again, red and swollen. This time it occurred after I'd been ill with a fever and infection from a cat scratch. Was it related to dehydration? Stress? Just a more acute flare of the arthritis that plagued my knees? Again I was overwhelmed with fear. What if I could not work, provide for myself?

Sometimes in these months, my will to die seemed greater than my will to live. I knew this was the depression of grief. I had to put it down, this burden of grief. I couldn't keep carrying it; it pulled me too close to the edge of Darkness.

The doctor still didn't know what was going on with my foot but put me on steroids again. She referred me to a rheumatologist, but the doctor couldn't tell anything after the attack had passed. Soon I was better and back at work. Fear and my work ethic were my prime motivators. Those didn't seem too noble, but I guess I should be grateful for whatever kept me going.

This Mother's Day, John and I went to Sewanee again. It was Megan's graduation with an MFA degree in Creative Writing. It was only a few days past Millie's second birthday, and we also learned that Megan was pregnant again. I was grateful for a good trip with John.

Glimpse of a thought that morning, that God loves me. Always so hard for me to think, remember, much less feel that. Guess I had felt so undeserving, so unimportant. I tried to remember the keystone of my earlier training: God loves me and has a wonderful plan for my life.

Later that month, John told me that the fund was out of money, and my fear elevated to panic. I was terrified that he would not have the money to pay for his medications and that everything we had done would be for naught. His co-insurance (Medicare supplement) cost $650 per month. His rent was $700. His Disability income was $950. His Medicare, which continued for three years after the transplant, didn't cover prescriptions or co-pays for all his doctor visits, labs, and Coumaden clinic. I had barely enough money to cover my own expenses.

John had continued to look regularly for jobs. He searched and applied online to no avail. The economy was only just beginning to pull out of recession. Finally he learned of an opportunity with an ambulance company, and for a few weeks he was able to help transport patients to dialysis. Staff at his former dialysis center were amazed to see him, how well he looked. He was grateful for the chance to give back even though the job didn't last. He kept looking.

I knew that many people were still praying for John, and for me, even though we didn't update the CarePages anymore. People remembered who he was, his strength, his will to live, even though they maybe didn't know how grave his difficulties still were.

Maybe because we were both so private, and struggling just to keep going, neither of us advertised how hard everything was, not even to each other. But we knew. Sometimes it was hard not to resent that all the friends who showed up in the crises didn't come or call anymore.

John—Hell, Spring, Year Four

Some of my memories are hard to find. I have to be in the right state of mind to dig deep enough for them. It's strange how some of the most painful times stay on the insides of my eyelids and are there as soon as I close my eyes. While others I don't think I'll ever remember at all.

I do remember what I thought was maybe Hell, when I was coming off being intubated the first time. There wasn't any fire or devil with horns and a tail, which I guess I had come to picture as Hell through childhood cartoons and Sunday school lessons, but it was an unforgiving, constant and eternal feeling of fear, loneliness, and claustrophobia. The feeling of eternity was worse than any pain or fear I experienced. It wasn't that I had been there for a long time and would be for a longer time, it was that there was no other time. No other place that I came from or could return to. It was pain and torture and fear that was without beginning or end and more intense than I can explain. There was no "real life," no Heaven, no Hell; only anguish.

After waking up I felt I had been away for an impossible amount of time. In my mind it seemed like thousands of years, and yet I believe just being there for a few seconds would have given me the same impression. If I had died at that point would I still be there? Was it Hell?

John—Infinity

For as long as I can remember, my fear of death hasn't been the moment itself but what comes next. For starters, I don't even know if I believe in Heaven or Hell. Nor do I know which one I would end up in if they do exist. And if they do exist but you don't believe in them, will you be assigned to one anyway?

As a kid, I pictured my maternal grandfather (who died three weeks after I was born) sitting up on a cloud looking down at his family left on Earth, or hanging out with his friends and family already in heaven. I prayed that he would look over me and that someday I would be able to meet him. When that day came, I figured I would do the same and watch over my remaining family from a floating cloud above them. But what would I do when everyone I knew on earth was dead and I had no entertainment? What would I do for eternity? I tried to wrap my young mind around being in heaven even after there was no Earth. It became so common that I taught myself to quit thinking about eternity/infinity completely, and to this day it freaks me out to think about being a bodiless consciousness floating through space for millions of years with no focus or purpose. I can see why some people believe in reincarnation, but even that would last forever.

Tonight, while attempting a meditation practice of envisioning white light flowing into the top of my head and towards any body parts in pain, as suggested by the voice talking to me through headphones, I couldn't help but wonder where that healing white light is supposed to come from. Being as it's healing, white, and from above, I wondered if it was from God or heaven, and immediately quit seeking it because I don't know if I deserve that. Who gets to make that call? And if God thought I shouldn't be in that pain, would He not fix it himself? What if my headache was his "plan" for me in the first place? I've never understood the concept that God has a plan for us yet we still can make our own decisions. Is there a purpose in praying for Him to show you your planned path? If it's planned by God, will it not happen anyway?

And to those who say God will never give you more than you can handle, have you talked to anyone suicidal? I haven't. But I think I can grasp where some of them are coming from. For most of my life I thought suicide was the most selfish thing imaginable and just wished whoever did it would do it in their bathtub so it'd be easier to clean up. That was before everyone in my family put their jobs on the line, lives on hold, and body on an operating table. Not to mention emotional and monetary support. I can now respect the idea of unburdening others. Of course it would be hard for them at first, and of course that's not what they want, but it's okay for a soldier to jump on a grenade to allow his friends to keep living their lives as planned. I'm not suicidal, but I'm not going to say it hasn't crossed my mind. And anyone who says he's never thought about it is a liar or narcissistic to the core. I've never gotten into the specifics of how to do it, but I have thought of how it could benefit my family.

I struggled for a long time wondering why I saw and felt so much pain and suffering and visions of what Hell might be like for me without any glimpse of white lights or a booming voice telling me it's going to be okay, that it's not my time. Anything to give me proof of something other than Hell. This was until I realized that I saw love and caring and faith and hope every day in the people around me, regardless of how scared they were. It came not only from family and friends who drove hours just to sit in my room while I was unconscious, but doctors holding my hands and praying with tears running down their faces, and nurses quietly talking to me, bathing me, and braiding my hair, knowing that I couldn't hear them and would most likely never know who they were. Maybe that's what they mean when they say you have to have faith.

Allison—Summer, Year Four

End of June, my family gathered in Atlanta for my birthday. Megan arranged it and even kept it a surprise that my cousin Diane was coming from Florida. After visiting the Botanical Gardens, we all went to my cousin Elaine's house where her children and grandchildren joined us. Sixteen people altogether came, just because they wanted to wish me a happy birthday. It reminded me of my thirtieth birthday, which I had always said was my favorite. Then, we had just moved back to Greenville and I was pregnant with John. That time the cookout was in the backyard of Elaine's and Diane's parents' house, and my parents were still living. Elaine and Diane each had two children, and Megan was happy swinging on the swings with her second cousins. It seemed like it was a simpler time. Today was almost as good.

At my insistence, John applied for Medicaid, and for months I dogged the process of trying to get his application approved. He had to send in more paperwork and finally in September, we learned that he had been denied. Because his father and I had helped at times, contributing what we could, Medicaid had considered this as income.

In the process of trying to get him approved, he and I had had become passionate about the need for Medicaid Expansion, which our state had refused. We agreed to be a part of a video that the South Carolina Hospital Association was producing for a grassroots and social media campaign. We told our story on camera for four hours—of which they would use only minutes. It was maybe the most we had talked about it together. Then the videographer followed us to a nearby playground at the elementary school that I, and both my children, had attended.

Standing on the new balcony looking down at the field, I watched John throw a ball to Pip. He looked *so normal*, lean and lanky, so *himself*, that for the first time I felt that he might be okay.

Every time I looked into my second bedroom, I saw John lying there sick. The ghosts of those memories stirred the fear and loneliness around my heart. I so loved my kids and yet I couldn't hold them close, keep them safe, make everything right in their lives. I sat in the armchair that used to be in Megan's room at our old house and I cried.

So on Labor Day weekend I bought a daybed with a trundle, and John helped me move the double bed out to the shed. It looked like a different room. I told him that if he needed to move back in with me, we could switch the beds again. I knew he wanted more than anything to be able to remain in his own place.

Allison—Fall, Year Four

I had resumed spiritual direction, something I had done in the past, with my friend Catherine. Her ministry through The Anchorage had been an anchor for me the past dozen years when church had not been a comfortable place. (Divorcing a minister tended to do that.) I confided my obsessive worry about John that never went away, regardless of some good times. I was ashamed when I told her how much I feared—that when he didn't respond to a text within a short period of time, I thought that he was dead. That every morning I woke up with fear at my throat. I said, "The world is not a safe place." She encouraged me to keep talking through the trauma, and she would be with me.

I went with her for a day trip to Mepkin Abbey near Charleston. Mepkin rested on the former estate of Claire Boothe Luce overlooking the Cooper River. I paused at the foot of a statute of Mary before joining Catherine on a bench near the river to eat our lunch. I noticed a small boat with a young man, an older man, and a dog that looked like Pip. I heard them laughing as they navigated near the shore. I prayed that vision for John; his love for the Charleston coast had always been as great as mine. I prayed that he might be that happy, healthy, and living a life he enjoyed.

I *had* to believe in God's goodness and his provision of care for me. How else could I live? Otherwise, life was too scary and uncertain to survive. As God commanded the waves and tides, so, I believed, He commanded the currents of my life. *Thy grace is sufficient.*

Then I was sick again, with an upper respiratory infection that approached pneumonia. As always when I was sick, the depression came back on me.

Reading a review of *The Trauma of Everyday Life* in the Sunday paper, I purchased the book and started reading. The author related how the Buddha, born into a life of privilege, choosing to spend years immersing himself among the poor, wrote about illness, suffering, aging, and death as "the experience of groundlessness" and about finding a way to make it nourishing rather than frightening. "Have an attitude toward the world that is at once realistic and hopeful," and learn to "tolerate the traumatic truth: All that arises is subject to cessation."

The book rang true with me, but I didn't know how to make my experience of the earth shifting "nourishing." I shared the book with John, who had read voraciously since his confinement.

I started seeing a counselor through our Employee Assistance Program, as well as continuing the spiritual direction. For both these services, I paid only a minimum amount or I would not have been able to do them. Money was a constant fear.

Those days I felt as though I was in mourning. Most days I wore black, no jewelry. It was not really a conscious decision. I didn't want to call attention to myself; it just didn't matter. I knew that I was still grieving so many losses, the shock of John's illness was still too present, the uncertainty of the future too prevailing. In social groups, it was hard to talk so I was even quieter than usual. I thought that I must be dull, disinteresting, drab. The fatigue was always there. I thought that only God and time could heal this tiredness. I pulled further into my shell. The only thing I could do was write, the only thing that seemed meaningful, and something I'd avoided for over a decade.

I had lots of dreams. One was particularly vivid.

I am driving to pick up John as a child and there's a traffic backup. Then I get word—cell phone?—that there's been a building collapse and John is under it. I drive down a parking ramp, under the building, forcing my way, telling officials there's a little boy trapped there, frightened and crying. They tell me there's radon everywhere, but I go where they lead me, now on foot, fearful and climbing over near-impossible obstacles. Then I am at the wall John is behind. I call to him and his crying stops. I keep talking and then reading books while they work to clear him out. Then his father arrives and insurance people are already signing over settlements for his injuries, damages. Then he is free and walks out. He is fine, no injuries at all.

Maybe my mind was still trying to work it all out. I prayed it would all end that well.

On the morning of November 5, John and I hurried to Chattanooga, but we didn't make it ahead of the baby who came fast. We were an hour away when my son-on-law called to say that I had another granddaughter. They were calling her by my first name. At the hospital, I held the miracle of baby Jane and then spent several days with their little family back in Sewanee. John's father took him back to Greenville. I was happy about all the blessings, but so aware of the tenuousness of John's situation and the pains of my own body. My knees wouldn't let me carry two-year-old Millie up the stairs and I was constantly tired.

We had been back at Sewanee only a couple of hours when my cell phone rang, an unknown number. I answered, and it was the woman from the state Medicaid office telling me that John's application had been approved. Trembling, I called John and told him, and then I told the others about this miracle. I had recently decided that I would keep paying his secondary insurance by putting it on my credit card. We had not resubmitted his application after it had been turned down two months earlier. Other than an act of God, the only reason I could think of was that someone in power saw the video of John's story. Now his medications would be covered! I breathed easier as I held baby Jane.

Back at home, I learned that John and his roommate, a friend for many years, had had a conflict and the roommate had moved out. Another job attempt and another relationship had not worked out. Besides the personal elements, his financial situation was even more stressed. I offered for him to move back in with me but he refused. He verbalized that he was lonely, that he had no friends, career, mate, or money. My heart broke, and there was nothing I could do.

On Saturday morning, December 14, John called me around 10:30. He was having shoulder/chest/underarm pain. Of course I immediately thought "heart" and wanted to take him to the emergency room. He refused, didn't even want me to call Dr. Skaggs. Finally he asked, "Do you think it could be Wegener's?"

The word seemed to come from the gates of hell. "What? Why would you think that?" I asked.

"You know—when I was having that bad shoulder pain? I was having to sleep with my arm over my head?"

Then there was the flashback: his leaving the internist's office in crazed pain, me going to get prescriptions filled for strong narcotics. His being admitted through the ER the next morning . . . .

I tried to breathe and then said, "Well, if it is, then you are seeing the best possible person on Tuesday." I offered to bring him something to eat and asked if there was anything else I could do.

I prayed, tried to quell my panic. It could be anything. I had known for weeks that he had not been well and had tried to get him help. The stress of finances, broken friendships, anxiety about trying to get work—none of these things were any good for auto-immune conditions. But he would see

Dr. Allen on Tuesday; I would go and drive him up on Monday. I fought against my own fears. I didn't think I could live through it again. Either God would overcome or John would succumb to this disease. There was nothing I could do. I went out and finished the shopping, got the gifts that must be mailed in time for Christmas.

The next day, John was better. He thought it could be the antibiotic causing the joint pain and rash. We went out for brunch. It was the third Sunday of Advent, Joy Sunday, and Megan's birthday, and the sun was out.

At 9 a.m., December 17, we were waiting in 2C, Duke South, the Transplant Center. John had had labs drawn. His rheumatology appointment was in the afternoon. His pain and rash were worse; he had not slept for three nights. Oddly, I didn't have a bad feeling about John's illness. People must have been praying for me.

At 2, John went in to see Dr. Allen and I sat in the waiting room of 1J. Finally Dr. Allen came out, John behind her, and motioned for me. I was always so glad to see her!

She said, "I think we are dealing with shingles."

She kept talking, but I didn't hear much more after that. I felt that my knees might give way. She left, John went to check out, and I dropped onto a bench to text Megan. Then I was crying and I could not stop. A woman stopped to ask if I was okay, and I nodded. Then John came up and asked, too. I couldn't speak for crying. He saw me holding my phone and said, "What is it? Is it Meg? Did somebody die?"

Finally I was able to say, "I'm just so happy."

He gave me a slightly disgusted look and grumbled, "It's not *that* good news. I have shingles!"

Then Megan texted and I relayed, "That's the best case of shingles I ever heard of!"

John shook his head at both of us and walked off toward the pharmacy. I picked up my things and followed. Relief unglued me and I felt like I could float or pass out, or both. We wouldn't be spending another near-Christmas with John hospitalized at Duke!

But back in Greenville, John was still sick and in pain. Emotionally exhausted, I started crying and left work early on Christmas Eve. It didn't feel like Christmas.

Later, I called John and took over soup and Duke's sandwiches. I didn't feel like going to church or our usual celebration at the Gowers. We each opened one present, per our tradition. He was able to come to my house the next day for lunch and presents. He seemed happy and left at 1 p.m. to go back to rest. I went to a movie and then supper with some friends.

On Boxing Day, December 26, all I could predict was that I would write this year.

A thought crossed my mind: I could ask to not have to feel or witness so closely all that John had to go through. I was not sure if it was really okay to ask that. It was such a mother thing. I would ask Mother Mary to intervene.

Leaving the gym, I saw a friend I'd known for nearly thirty years. He asked about John, and I filled in some details.

He said, "You are turning into a saint! I never saw that coming."

I responded, "I don't want to be!"

I was rather offended by both his observations, characterization, of me past and present. But here I was: "poverty, chastity, sanctity." How did I get here? All I knew was that "mother" love was my strongest, deepest force, and that I could and was willing to be present with John through all this, when others could not or would not. How could I not be changed?

Though I worried about my lack of faith, I found comfort in I Corinthians 13:13: ". . . faith, hope and love. But the greatest of these is love."

So I kept doing what I had done every morning for a dozen years, praying what was known as the Third Step Prayer: *God, I offer myself to Thee, to build with me and do with me as Thou wilt. Relieve me of the bondage of self that I may better do Thy will. Take away my difficulties that victory over them may bear witness to those I would help of Thy power, Thy love, and Thy way of life. May I do Thy will always.*

Allison—Winter, Year Four

January, my least favorite month, was of course cold and dark. I was grateful for the cocoon of my bed and soft, fluffy blanket this morning, for not waking to the sound of rain. I had the virus that was going around. My immunities had been weakened by the stress of these years. I feared that my co-workers would think I was not doing a good enough job.

At the end of the month, we got snow again. I was aware of the quiet in the early hours, with the snow a blanket. It was not too bad and I made it in to work by 11 a.m.

John's friend invited him to upstate New York, in view of a job there with his stepfather. He had bought John a plane ticket for twelve days. I was afraid for him to go but knew that he needed to do something. I offered to drive him to the Charlotte airport, thinking that the air trip would be hard enough, and also that the cost of leaving his truck in airport parking would be significant.

I was awake at 5 a.m. when John called to make sure that I was up, and I picked him up at 6 a.m. I could tell he was both excited and anxious. Because of his recent years of illness, he had not flown in years and never by himself that I recalled. I thought about how different his experiences had been from his sister's. I prayed this would be something good for him. I told him to watch for angels.

Inside, I waited to watch him go through the security check. He turned and waved and walked on where I could not go. It was like seeing my four-year-old head off to the first day of kindergarten, only ten times worse.

He texted later that he had to run for his connection in Atlanta and was pretty wiped out when he got on the second plane, but he made it. His friend picked him up at the New York airport and they drove another two hours to Ithaca. He was happy and excited.

By the next day, he learned there was no job. We never knew the exact details about all that, but he worked during those days plowing and shoveling show. He was ready to come home.

A couple of days before his return flight, we got predictions of heavy snow for the Greenville-Charlotte area. I knew I wouldn't be able to drive to the airport to get him on Tuesday. I called his father who said the snow would be worse for them, and that John would just have to stay in the airport or get to a motel until someone could eventually get him. I knew he couldn't do that; it would be too taxing for him. Again I was distraught, so tired of never having anyone to help or enough money for any alternative.

Late Sunday afternoon, John texted that he had found another flight straight into Greenville leaving early Monday and arriving ahead of Tuesday's predicted snow. I put the airfare on my credit card. I worried that he wouldn't be able to get to the airport there, but he made the early-morning flight out of New York. I was relieved when he arrived safely back in Greenville Monday afternoon. His situation had not changed, but he had tried an alternative and come back none the worse.

The snow hit—twelve inches. It was the most snow we'd had in decades. Greenville shut down and I stayed in for two days. I was afraid we would lose power; my neighbor came over to light my gas logs in case I needed them. The snow reminded me of the time twenty-plus years ago when the kids were little and we first got to know the Gowers. We were snowed in almost ten days that time. So many things have changed since then.

John continued to look diligently for jobs. His father helped him pay his rent since he was without a roommate. He was depressed, and I worried obsessively.

In a counseling session as I was talking about my worry over the future, the counselor, looking almost puzzled, asked me, "Where is your faith?"

"I don't know!" I burst out. It was such a fair and obvious question. Where was my faith? Where did it go? Why could I not trust the God who had provided for us continuously to do so in the future? I wished I had an answer.

John—Punishment, Karma, Prayer/Religion

Despite being born the son and grandson of preachers, growing up going to church, and generally knowing better, it was hard not to feel like I was being punished. Did God "give" me this terrible disease because of sins I had committed? Or was that more along the lines of karma? Although I didn't consider myself a "bad" person, I had committed more than my fair share of sinning and was hardly what anyone would consider innocent.

There are many things I don't understand about religion. Why do children and innocents suffer and die? Why are the people who commit atrocities seemingly rewarded? And on the other hand, why are some tortured and killed solely for their belief in a God who sits back and watches them suffer?

I became frustrated with it all, especially prayer. I've always prayed. Every night for as long as I remember I at least say, "Dear Lord, please forgive me for my sins." Please help others to forgive me and me to forgive others for the sins we have committed. Please be with my family and friends and forgive them for their sins. Keep them healthy and let them know they are loved." From there I usually pray for specific things for each member of my family and when I can't sleep, I list all of my aunts, uncles, cousins, nieces, and nephews. Some people may have a problem with the semantics of my prayer, but I don't care. I can't even remember how old I was when I started saying it.

My point is I've always prayed regardless of the questions and doubts in my mind. My mom, dad, stepmom, and grandparents have all studied and/or taught religion and have been there to answer my questions without forcing beliefs down my throat. I've always been grateful for this and the thousands of prayers for me while I was in the hospital. But after a while, it became hard for me to hear "well so and so is praying for you." So what? I have tubes shoved in every hole in my body plus a few extra, I'm tired, I'm thirsty, I'm hungry, I'm in indescribable pain, I might not ever get out of this bed again. But hey, at least Susie Q. in Georgia is praying for me. At one point my frustration with everything boiled over when my mom told me that somebody I'd never heard of was praying for me and I said, "Will you tell her to make me a sandwich instead?"

It sounds like I'm an ungrateful, insincere heretic and I am probably more nervous about what people think reading this than any other personal details I've written. The power of prayer isn't lost on me. It was always uplifting to know that people were thinking of me and that people cared, but I never could grasp my mother's belief level that these prayers were going to be the difference in me living or dying. The only thing she could do while I was dying was pray. And she prayed constantly. But is life so trivial that prayer is the difference in living or dying? If one church accidentally left me off the prayer list would I have a bad night? If the girl walking by herself with her IV pole down the hall every day doesn't have people praying for her, while I did the same with my family and friends cheering each step and taking pictures to share online, would God think differently of her? I thought she was the bravest person I saw in the hospital.

There was one prayer that I remember well. I'm not sure what the hospital policy is about staff praying with patients but you can bet your ass when your top doctors come to your bedside and ask to pray with you, it's not because things are looking up. When Dr. Kirakoula held my hand and prayed, it was comforting and scary. She's up there with the sweetest and smartest doctors I've ever met and I trusted her 100 percent. If she told me I'd be cured by jumping out of the hospital window, I would've asked her to roll my bed over there. I don't remember a single word she said but I remember the significance. It was desperation. She had become close to my family and me. She was the person we went to for answers and she was saying she didn't have any more. The doctors had showed their hand. She was a concerned friend now and had nothing left to do but pray. We both cried as she finished and tried not to say goodbye.

A couple of years after getting out of the hospital, on a particularly bad day, I was extremely depressed. Life wasn't back to normal, and I wasn't sure if there would ever be a normal again. My mom said, "Maybe you were supposed to die there. Maybe it's my fault for praying so hard that you're still alive and unhappy." Since then I've tried to be less of a burden to her. At the time I think I told her I doubted she had that kind of sway with the Man Upstairs.

Although she may not have saved my life with her prayers, she most definitely saved my life. Even without taking one of her kidneys, I may not have lived without her help.

Allison—Spring, Year Five

On Easter Sunday, John went with me to Earle Street Baptist Church. He looked so handsome in his spring suit. I was pleased and proud. I remembered how people had referred to him as "Lazarus" when he almost died at Duke. I was also reminded of a comment made recently by a friend regarding John: "He has a heavy cross to bear."

He'd begun working some, back at the company where he worked before he got sick. He was glad to have something to do, although it was not what he wanted and there were no benefits. Other than the hospitalizations, not working these years was what he hated most.

This year, John and I did the annual Kidney Walk together. We talked with other recipients and their families, and he saw some of his former dialysis clinicians. It was amazing—this segment of life that I never even knew to think about—and now we were part of it. John continued to express interest in working for LifePoint, the organ procurement group.

That night, the tired, lonely feeling was back. It was the shadow of the trauma graying me, probably from talking and remembering. I wanted to run from it. I journaled:

I have the sense today that the terror might be behind us. As I am psychically half-crouched, exhausted, waiting for the next blow, the next tremor of the earth, glancing about to see if John escaped or if he needs me . . . I have the awareness that maybe it is over. Maybe there is life for a while. John is working some again, building up stamina days at a time, back at his old job. He wants to play soccer again.

My sense suddenly is to RUN, FORWARD—toward life, away from the dark dangers of the past four years; run away from the timidity and inertia that has held me in abeyance to John's impending life-and-death needs. The farther I get from the past years' trauma, the stronger I will become. Run, forward. Run, and don't look back. Yet it is really hard to do that.

On Mother's Day, John went to church with me again. I stood when all the mothers were recognized. I was almost overcome and felt that I would break down. I was so aware that I almost lost him, of how different this day would be if he were not here. There was also a baby dedication, and I remembered John's thirty years ago. We had dedicated him to God then. I had to trust that God's will was being done in his life. I thought that maybe I could find in this place some of the "family" I experienced in my church growing up, and how it had always been such a source of strength for me.

I was back at the orthopaedist, getting X-rays of my knees and also having him check my foot, which still periodically flared with pain and inflammation. He told me that the arthritis in my knees was worse and that the foot was tendonitis. Then, less than two weeks later, my right hand suddenly hurt, swelled, and I couldn't move it. It was a Tuesday night and I had just gone to bed. The pain was so bad I couldn't sleep. Finally I got up around 3 a.m., thinking I would take a bath, anything to relieve my hurting. Then I realized I couldn't get out of the bathtub. There was still a handgrip on the side of the tub, but it was on the right side and I couldn't use my right hand.

Fear overwhelmed me. *This is what it has come to, what it will be like. I am helpless, I won't be able to work, I won't be able to live alone.* I forced myself to make my knees push me up, despite pain, and got out. I took a couple more Tylenol and made it to morning when I called my friend and administrator at the hospital.

"Can you get me in to the orthopaedist quick? And can you come get me?" I asked. "I can't drive." All I could think was to get a cortisone shot. She worked her magic and called back to say she would be at my house by 8 a.m.; he would see me first thing.

She had to open the car door for me; I couldn't use my hand at all. In the doctor's office, after more X-rays, he did not know what was causing the problem. He tried to inject a steroid but it would not even release into my hand. He gave me prescriptions for 30 milligrams of oral steroid for several days and for a painkiller.

My friend had waited for me and drove me back to Greenville. She would have to cover my responsibilities—a significant photo shoot—that day. She only commented, "You are not going to be able to sleep for days!"

My doctor got me an appointment to see the rheumatologist the next day. I took the steroids and one pain pill and slept for hours. The next morning, my hand was some better and I was able to drive myself to the rheumatologist who scolded me for not coming to her first.

I cried in her office, telling her about my feeling of helplessness. She was solicitous, assuring me I would be all right. She thought my hand, and the flare-ups in my foot, were gout or pseudo-gout. I had none of the indicators for gout, other than that my father had had it. I knew John would think it had to do with giving the kidney. She started me on a preventive medication.

I slept most of the next three days, without even taking any pain pills after the first one. Not having to surface for work, I was living in the deepness. I called my daughter and told her of my desperation. She said I could always come live in her guest room. I couldn't imagine ever doing that, but her saying it afforded me some sort of absolute in my downward slide.

On Saturday I saw a friend who spoke harshly to me. When I whined about my loneliness and my fear, she said, "You want your God to have skin. The real One doesn't!" I spend the evening writing about how powerless I was over things in my life. Then I read and tried to meditate on how all-powerful and all-loving God is. To not think everything is up to me.

My friend Catherine told me that the Abbot at Mepkin said, "We are praying for Allison in her darkness."

"I don't want to be in darkness!" I responded.

She assured me, "No one thinks you do. You are doing the work. It is in God's time."

The next day I hosted a jewelry party for a friend at my house. I had promised weeks before, and I didn't want to renege. She took a picture of me, saying I looked so pretty. I kept the photo, seeing only the hurt in my eyes and the vulnerability in my face, the look of a wounded animal. But by evening I felt much better, for getting out of myself. The next day I was ready for the work week, to pick up and start again.

My grass, dormant for the winter, did not come back this spring. After all our toil, my front lawn was withered and brown.

6

Healing

Allison—Summer, Year Five

IN JUNE I JOINED a Sunday School class. I had met the minister through The Anchorage, and he had been incredibly kind—enough to get me back into a church again. The class, recommended to me, was small and all women. I didn't know anyone. After they introduced themselves, the teacher asked me to tell them a little about myself. Surprisingly, I said, "I may cry."

They assured me that would be perfectly fine. I said a bit about my son's sudden illness, what the past few years had been like, and then, sure enough, I was crying. I was shocked at myself, but it was not worth it anymore to simply say I was fine. I felt their support and they prayed for me. Through this class, and my writing, healing was beginning. Actually, I knew that healing had been ongoing. All of the processing, all of the phases and stages, had been essential parts of the journey.

After lunch, I decided to drive up to the mountains, toward Asheville. I remembered the drive there to get John, and the consequent emergency room experience and harrowing drive back at midnight. But today was beautiful, sunny and warm. Randomly, I exited at Flat Rock and drove toward the camp where Megan spent so many summers. Again, many memories. They were of a simpler time.

I ended up at Highland Lake Inn, without intention. I couldn't remember the name of it when I first thought to look for it. Then I was driving up the graveled road beside the waterfall. I had first come here for Leadership Greenville retreats twenty-plus years ago and later brought the family back for weekends. I parked and went to lie in one of the hammocks. A few families were about. I heard their laughter and again remembered happier times. I was glad we had the money then to do some nice things.

After a while, I walked down toward the lake. I noticed on my left a statue that I'd never seen before. It seemed odd, standing in an expanse of green hillside. I approached it and saw that it was the Virgin Mary. Her back was to the path and she was facing one of the Inn's vegetable gardens. All white, she was full sized and stood on a pedestal, tall above me. Her arms were outstretched. I remembered all the times at Duke that I prayed for her intercession. Looking up, I saw streaks of lighted sky at her head. I touched her left hand with my right and asked her to please take away my pain over John. I felt tears rise again. I turned and walked on to the lake's edge.

Gazing out over the water to the tall trees surrounding it, I prayed that my sorrows be removed from me, that I might lift the black cloud and let it disperse over the lake. I felt more tears and turned away to walk back, still heavy with sadness. Seeing Mary in the distance, I sat on a picnic bench at the lake's edge.

Suddenly I was face-to-face with my trauma, at the root of my sadness. I saw myself sitting in the Duke ICU waiting room and a chaplain saying that I looked like Mary in the Pieta. At that moment, I remembered clearly how I felt in those hours, when the fear was greatest that John would die. Suddenly I was sobbing, what I couldn't do in that waiting room. My head on the picnic table, I realized that a part of me still and always had thought that John was dying. I saw the sharp reality of that false thought. FEAR: False Evidence Appearing Real. And I had never been able to go back fully and look, see the lie. How all along, a part of me had been with John *in dying*, refusing to trust in his living, waiting for the postponed suspension to end. That was why the pain had been so great, the hurt so deep, that I have wondered if I could live. And it was all about fear and not reality. I had still been in the waiting room, frozen in fear, stuck between fight and flight, waiting to hear the pronouncement that he was dead.

Finally, slowly, I walked back to Mary and on her other side, touched her right hand. I thanked her for hearing me.

I was able to go to the beach for a weekend, to stay with my friend Ellen. I hadn't been to the beach since John got sick, nor seen Ellen much in the past two years. I hadn't had the energy but to work and to hide, and she had had changes in her own life. I didn't know what I would feel like doing. My knees limited my activities.

The time with her was just like it used to be, only maybe better. We talked a lot, and Ellen, always active, kept me moving. On Saturday there was a long walk on the beach and then dinner out with her friend Alice. Afterward, Alice came back to the house with us for a celebration of the summer solstice. She led us through some rituals, including one in which we lit a rolled-up piece of tissue paper that was standing on a card. I went first. My tissue tower burned for a moment and then flopped over, dying out. I was disturbed but didn't say anything. Then Ellen and Alice lit theirs and they lifted and flew!

Finally I verbalized that my tissue didn't have a good foundation and therefore not enough support. Alice commented, "We speak in metaphor when we don't even realize it."

Groundlessness. Earthquake. The ground shifting beneath me. I heard these phrases in my head. I had lost my footing these years, and it was a terrible struggle regaining it. Alice reminded me of my first, or root, chakra, and I half-remembered ages-old truths I used to know.

On Sunday, we went on a long bike ride from Isle of Palms to the other end of Sullivan's Island and there I paddle boarded! I didn't stand up, but I am amazed that I could actually do something again and have fun. Then we biked all the way back to Isle of Palms.

Back at home, I got out my book about chakras and read again, particularly about the first chakra which symbolized security, stability, the earth. I also read about the tenth, which is an individual's energy below the surface of the earth. I liked this thought; my energy goes deep below the ground's shifting surface. I practiced some of the meditations and I felt stronger.

I also returned to my roots of reading the Bible (Psalms) every morning, in addition to my devotional books and prayer.

I began to notice that I was not waking with fear. I didn't remember exactly when it stopped.

In July I went back to the rheumatologist. She kept me on preventive medication for the gout-like condition and also gave me a steroid shot in each knee. In less than a day, I realized that I was without pain for the first time in several years. It was amazing how much brighter my attitude was without pain in my body. Again, I was mindful of how John must feel every day.

In August, Ellen graciously allowed the six of us – John, Megan and her family, and me—to use her beach house for several days. It was the first real vacation I'd had had for years. I watched John swim in the ocean and remembered the times that all he wanted was to go to the beach again. His life was a continuing miracle.

I sat with Megan under the beach umbrella and watched the two little girls playing in a shallow tidal pool. When all the horror started with John, these two little ones weren't even here.

Late summer John and I went again to Sewanee, this time for baby Jane's baptism. He was the chauffeur, for which I was immensely grateful. John was well and everyone commented on how good he looked.

I remembered once, about a year ago, when he was having one difficulty after another, and I said, "It's all going to be okay."

He turned to look at me, squarely, and said, "I never thought it wouldn't be."

This last day of summer, I went out to get my newspaper. The sweetness of tea lilacs scented the crisp air. I looked out over my grass, now thick and green. I had taken soil samples, learned that it had a fungus, treated it several times with a fungicide. And it had come back, blade by blade, over the months.

It has been more than four years since John got sick. I thought about the people, young, old, and middle-aged, who had died during these years, and yet John lived. I still had worries for him. He hadn't been able to get a fulltime job with benefits. I worried how he would afford the health care he needs. But thus far, God provided.

John—Gym, Fall, Year Five

After two miles on the elliptical (in about 30 minutes), I moved on to the weights. Leg day. Before I got sick it was my favorite workout of the week. Since, it's been my least and the most difficult.

Four-plus years since getting sick and after almost three with my mom's kidney, I'm finally starting to notice a difference on leg day. Finally noticing muscle coming back to the sticks I've used for legs these past years.

The best and worst part of working out is running. Or elliptical-ing in my case. Today, beside the hottest girl in the gym (running twice as fast as I on the treadmill), I did what I always do. Push myself until my lungs start burning, I'm audibly sucking air, sweating through my shirt, and remembering. Remembering the fear of not being able to breathe. Remembering the machines blowing air in to me to the point I couldn't talk, eat, drink, or sleep. One of the scariest moments of my life has become the perfect motivation. It might not be the best look next to the gorgeous brunette on mile 12 (and still gorgeous), but hey, you do what you gotta do.

John—More about Doctors

I've felt pretty good for the last few weeks. It's my favorite time of year; my birthday is near, college football has started, and the heat of southern summer is releasing its sweaty grip.

Driving my mom up to Sewanee for Jane's baptism this past weekend, I finally learned the name of my favorite ICU nurse at Duke, Zeliah. I thought I remembered asking Mom and them not knowing; must have been a dream.

Jane's godmother is Megan's friend Susan, who was in medical school when I started getting sick and was the first person to suggest Wegener's when hearing about my symptoms. She has gone on to become a rheumatologist and to work with Wegener's patients.

The night before the baptism, after going over my current medications with her, she mentioned having five years left with my mom's kidney. The shock of the matter-of-fact comment almost knocked me out of my chair. We were both drinking dirty vodka martinis, so my immediate thought was that she must've gotten her facts mixed up or I heard her wrong. Half a thought later my brain was off to the races, searching through the millions of bits of medical information I'd heard since I'd got sick, to figure out what she was talking about. After what felt like an hour, I remembered reading somewhere that the average life of a transplanted kidney is something like seven-to-eight years. It was one of those facts I must've tried to forget. Along with the fact that most people with Wegener's have multiple flare-ups with varying degrees of severity throughout their lives. Which was another topic of conversation with Susan.

It's been almost three years since the transplant and having four hours of dialysis three days a week. The thought of going back there was one of a million things going through my head when Susan was talking. Years ago, when Megan told me Susan decided to go to med school, I couldn't picture it. Susan was too nice and funny and caring to be a doctor. That one conversation changed my mind. Although still all of those things, she is definitely a doctor now. She has gained the uncanny power of throwing out facts or numbers with no thought of what personal impact they might have. In her defense, I think she meant it in a positive way.

Only a few of the hundreds of doctors I've come in contact with seemed to be consciously aware of how their words can affect on a patient. Of course they break bad news gently, but general conversation can be shocking. I'm sure dealing with death and bad news on a constant basis can be desensitizing, and I assume the ability to dehumanize it is taught, at least to some degree. Which honestly makes perfect sense. I consider it similar to soldiers being drilled to the point that muscle memory takes over and standard operating procedure will be followed with little conscious effort. If doctors or soldiers or anyone who deals with constant death and hectic situations tried to take the time to process the feelings of everyone involved, nothing would ever get done.

It's something I've thought about often and have heard many other patients and family members complain about. I definitely don't know the answer! Of course it would be great if all doctors and nurses took into account everyone's mindset before they spoke, and of course that would never happen. Would you rather your doctor spend one day a week in "personableness" workshops or in the OR practicing that one obscure skill that might save your life? That being said, there is a limit to how much patients should let them get away with. I had found mine with that nephrologist who was talking on his phone while taking out my chest tube.

7

Stasis

Allison—Fall, Year Eight

MORE THAN SEVEN YEARS since John got sick. "A new normal," cancer people call it, but nothing seems particularly normal. Every day is another jaunt of faith, wondering how God will show up today.

One thing Dr. Allen left off her list of possible outcomes that June day when John lay dying in Duke's ICU was depression. He has navigated all the others, including all the immune and gastro issues of infections and recurring C. diff, and even coming off long-term heavy narcotics cold turkey and alone. Those warrant remembering.

Two-plus years ago, in April of course, exactly five years since it began, John and I repeated the trip to the Baptist Easley emergency room. He had been sick all winter and had been put on various antibiotics again. Pale, weak and in severe pain, he'd lost another fifteen pounds. But that week we had both been invited to speak to the class of second-year medical students in Greenville about Wegener's, since it is such a rare disease and difficult to diagnose. John was excited about it and rewarded by the opportunity; the students, not much younger than he, were rapt at what he had been through. Partly because of John's experience (along with others', I'm sure), Rituxan is now the standard treatment for Wegener's and much less toxic than the previous Cytoxan. As our now-rheumatologist friend Susan tells us, Vanderbilt medical students come to her practice in Nashville knowing of John's case. Again, like at Duke, it was a rare time of validation for him when someone could understand.

However, he called me a couple of days later because he was too sick to get himself to the doctor. Thinking he would need IV fluids, I took him to the emergency room. There, they couldn't get a blood pressure at triage and he was rushed back to the critical care area. Before I could even get my head around this, a doctor was asking did I want him to be transferred to the Greenville hospital or to Duke. I quickly texted Dr. Skaggs, who made a call and then encouraged me to come to Greenville. Seemingly within minutes of my letting the ER doctor know, a nurse came to say that he would be admitted to 4005.

John and I both recognized the number, and he started crying.

"Why is he going to ICU?" I verbalized our question.

I was assured that he just needed to be under close surveillance, but we both knew better.

Then it was the exact drill as before: me calling his father and Megan and sobbing to co-workers with John in a frenzy of pain and fear. Following the ambulance to Greenville again, making the same phone calls to my cousins. Waiting in the ICU for doctors to say what was going on.

Sepsis, from a recurrence of the C. diff. I had to look up the definition. "Sepsis is a life-threatening complication of an infection causing injuries to organs and tissues." A bulletin board in the ICU proclaimed further information about its severity.

John's pain was unrelenting, as always, but particularly in his head and neck. Doctors were discussing doing a spinal tap to check for meningitis again. Megan was insisting by phone that we get him on to Duke. Vic and Janet were on the way to Greenville.

Except for the pain, getting massive doses of Dilaudid, and being treated like a junkie again, he pulled through and after 48 hours was transferred to a room. But this time in ICU, I refused to leave him, knowing the PTSD experience he suffered with that. I suffered my own consequences by acquiring C. diff myself the day he was released from the hospital.

As a result of the near-death sepsis, a wonderful doctor at Greenville got interested in John's case and insisted to Duke that John temporarily stop one immunosuppressant and cut the other in half. This doctor, a hematologist/oncologist, also questioned why John was still on Coumaden after five years, necessitating regular clinic checks and continued risk of bleeding, and he took him off that as well. With those changes, John's body began to have a chance to heal with no further ill effects.

The emotional, social, and financial issues remained.

That fall, with encouragement from this doctor, and possibly the remembered ordeal with pain control during that last hospitalization, John determined to take himself off the three strong narcotics he had been on since the beginning of his illness. And because of the experience in high school with inpatient treatment and his fear/dread of hospitalization in general, he refused to get help. I went to his place daily, where he was again alone, imagining that he would have died from seizures. This wonderful doctor also went by, more than once, to check on him and keep him hydrated. John did it own way, as he is wont to do. Except for a brief bout with sciatica, he has been free of all narcotics for nearly two years.

Depression has been another thing.

Megan sent me a PBS video about lengthy ICU stays titled, "Are patients coming out of ICU worse than when they went in?" I had it on in my car and started crying as I was driving down Augusta Road. The premise was that the "cocooning" of patients in long-term induced comas with heavy sedation has significant negative effects on brain chemistry. Again all my guilt rose that we had all done John more harm than good in our need to save him.

Thankfully, I know that is not true. John's will to live was unbeatable, as I believe is God's purpose for him to be alive, and well. But we all, society and the healthcare system alike, fall so short of helping people to truly heal from dastardly traumatic illnesses.

I had tried for two years to get John a psychiatrist appointment. Because he still gets Disability (which is periodically reviewed), he has Medicare and therefore he is better off than most. However, Medicare does not pay for outpatient services, and most psychiatrists will only accept private pay. After seven years, I was totally broke and doing all I could to help John live.

Another interesting fact is that the state of South Carolina does not provide any Medicare supplements for those under age 65. And while John has periodically been on Medicaid, which does help with medications and co-pays for any provider who will accept it, he usually is turned down because he makes too much money. "Too much money" is approximately $1,000 per month (which is his Disability).

This past January John was finally able to get in with a psychiatrist and get some help with the depression. A therapist was willing to see him pro-bono several times and made a couple of good suggestions on which Dr. Skaggs was able to help follow up. John has been able to get a part-time job with some regular income while continuing to explore career opportunities.

I have been trained to look at the whole person when offering help: physical, mental, emotional, spiritual and social. With John's experience, I learned that financial is a category just as important. My early professional training in social work/Christian social ministries, along with my work in hospitals for many years, has been a touchstone for me in helping John. I know that I have the knowledge and tools to figure this out; I am smart and definitely motivated—and it hasn't been enough.

In many ways, the physical was the easiest. John has been saved from illnesses that should have killed him. He was able to get the best medical care in the world. Mental and emotional issues were harder. Resources are limited and hard to access, even for someone searching for them. Spiritual has been a source of strength for me, but much more complicated for John. Social has been very difficult, and isolation becomes the fallback. But financial has been the worst, a daily struggle. I have continued to ask, or beg, for help. Good people have stepped up.

At the beach once again recently, John is tall and lean, happy and healthier than I've seen him in too many years. He has done what he loves: cruising the creeks on Smith's jon boat, dragging a line. He is better than I ever thought possible.

I am amazed and still somewhat holding my breath, but his strength is undeniable. It is born out of refining fires, tensile tested. He has survived; I pray he can thrive.

He sent us a picture and I see his toes stretched out toward the fishing poles. They are *his* feet, not the swollen clubs they were for a time. I guess I may never forget images like that. Maybe I don't want to. Without them I would not be the person I have become.

A Sunday School class member recently returned from a mission trip to Ecuador recounted that the area of their camp was formed by an earthquake. The new land, which hadn't existed before, now provided access to water from a higher ground.

"Sometimes you have to let the river run," the pastor there had said.

Ernest Hemmingway reflected on the "soul-wrenching challenges, as well as the transformative power of hardships. . . . The world breaks everyone, and afterward many are stronger at the broken places."

John will always have scars, on his body and his psyche, and conditions that he will have to manage. His voice is different, and the shape of his nose. I also have my scars. But we survived, and perhaps we are stronger, too. The gifts of healing can come in unexpected, even traumatic, circumstances.

For today, the tidal wave has passed.

John—August 2017

To say that I'm lucky wouldn't really describe my life. In fact, I am lucky to have the family, friends, and community that I do. But to say I am alive because of luck would not be fair to my family, friends, doctors, nurses, or myself. At no point did we give up. My mom, especially, refused to accept the situation in which I found myself, to the point of facing fear, uncertainty, and pain to help me. Although I don't remember some of what happened while I was hospitalized, I will never forget the difference of being in the hospital with and without my family. It was absolute night and day, and I don't doubt I would've died without them. I'll also never forget the friends who showed up while times were tough. When there was no music playing or beer being served, they walked in with tears in their eyes to see me again, not knowing if it would be the last time.

It didn't kill me and sure as hell didn't make me physically stronger, but I am a better person for it. If for no other reason than having a better understanding of pain and fear and hope and family and love. I am thankful for my life and everyone in it.

Sometimes, though, the progress almost seems like part of the problem. I feel so much better (AM so much better) and things still won't fall into place. I can't seem to get the job, money, relationships, depression, etc., to catch up. And it still feels like every time I make some progress, there's something there to slap me back down.

Going forward nonetheless, I hope to make people aware of the often unseen and misunderstood conditions involving autoimmune diseases, and I intend on doing everything I can to be an advocate for organ and tissue donation. If one person is able to donate an organ because of me, I may have figured out why I was given a second chance.

Every Day

Don't give up.
Be honest with myself and others.
Smile at them, in spite of.
Don't waste energy on anyone's negative opinion.
Keep thinking of the future.
It will all get better, even if it briefly gets worse.
Remember who loves you and those you love.

Questions for Discussion

- Autoimmune diseases, difficult to diagnose and understand
- Wegener's granulomatosis, or now Granulomatosis with Polyangitis
- Need for transplants; how to become an organ donor or a living kidney donor
- Need for Medicare coverage for life for renal patients to cover immunosuppressant medications
- Expanded Medicaid coverage
- Social networks for those with rare diseases and traumatic illnesses
- PTSD, or psychological trauma
- Ways a church or community can support individuals with chronic illness

Helpful Resources

Vasculitis Foundation, http://www.vasculitisfoundation.org/
National Kidney Foundation, https://www.kidney.org/
Donate Life America, https://www.donatelife.net/